75 BIBLE QUESTIONS

Your Instructors Pray You Won't Ask

Other books by Gary North
Marx's Religion of Revolution (1968, 1989)
An Introduction to Christian Economics (1973)
Puritan Economic Experiments (1974) [1988]
How You Can Profit from the Coming Price Controls (1974, 1976, 1977) [1978]
Unconditional Surrender (1981, 1983, 1988, 1994)
Successful Investing in an Age of Envy (1981) [1982] [1983]
The Dominion Covenant: Genesis (1982, 1987)
Government by Emergency (1983) [1991]
The Last Train Out (1983)
Backward, Christian Soldiers? (1984)
Coined Freedom: Gold in the Age of the Bureaucrats (1984, 1985)
Moses and Pharaoh (1985)
12 Deadly Nega-Trends (1985)
The Sinai Strategy (1986)
Conspiracy: A Biblical View (1986)
Honest Money (1986)
Fighting Chance (1986) [with Arthur Robinson]
Unholy Spirits: Occultism and New Age Humanism (1986) [1988] [1994]
Dominion and Common Grace: The Biblical Basis of Progress (1987)
Inherit the Earth (1987)
Liberating Planet Earth (1987)
Healer of the Nations (1987)
The Pirate Economy (1987)
Is the World Running Down? (1988)
When Justice Is Aborted (1989)
Political Polytheism (1989)
Social Security, The Coming Implosion (1988, 1989) [1991, 1993]
The Hoax of Higher Criticism (1990)
Tools of Dominion: The Case Laws of Exodus (1990)
Victim's Rights (1990)
The Judeo-Christian Tradition (1990)
Westminster's Confession (1991)
Christian Reconstruction (1991) [with Gary DeMar]
The Coase Theorem (1992)
Politically Incorrect (1993)
Salvation Through Inflation (1993)
Rapture Fever (1993)
Tithing and the Church (1994)
Leviticus: An Economic Commentary (1994)
Bills from Beyond the Grave (1995)
Baptized Patriarchalism (1995)
Lone Gunners for Jesus (1995)
Crossed Fingers (1996)

75 BIBLE QUESTIONS
Your Instructors Pray You Won't Ask

Gary North

Institute for Christian Economics
Tyler, Texas

Library of Congress Cataloging-in-Publication Data

North, Gary.
   75 Bible questions your instructors pray you won't ask / Gary North. -- 2nd ed.
      p. cm.
   Includes bibliographical references.
   ISBN 0-930462-03-3
   1. Dominion theology--Miscellanea. 2. Bible--Miscellanea. 3. Calvinism--Miscellanea.
   4. Predestination--Biblical teaching--Miscellanea. 5. Law (Theology)--Biblical teaching--Miscellanea. 6. Kingdom of God--Biblical teaching--Miscellanea. 7. Sociology, Christian (Reformed Church)--Miscellanea. I. Title.
   BT82.25.N66 1996
   230'.046--dc20   96-28357
                                                              CIP

Copyright © 1984, 1988
by Gary North

Second Edition, 1988
Third Printing, 1996

All rights reserved. Written permission must be secured from the publisher to use or reproduce any part of this book, except for brief quotations in critical reviews or articles.

Published by Institute for Christian Economics
P.O. Box 8000, Tyler, Texas 75711

Printed in the United States of America

This book is dedicated to

Bob and Rose Weiner

the founders of *Maranatha*, the "hardest core" campus ministry of this generation

Table of Contents

Introduction 1

PART I — Sovereignty: God's or Man's 13
Introduction to Part I 15

1. Didn't God Hate the Unborn Infant Esau? 17
2. Could Pharaoh Have Repented? 19
3. Does God's Absolute Predestination
   Make Him Unfair? 21
4. If We Can't Work Our Way INTO Salvation,
   How Can We Work Our Way OUT? 23
5. How Can God GUARANTEE Good for His
   People without PREDESTINATING Good? .. 25
6. How Can We Escape the Love of God? 27
7. If We Can "Fall from Grace," Isn't Christ's
   Intercession Ineffective? 29
8. Are We LESS than Conquerors? 31
9. Doesn't God Make "Vessels Fitted
   for Destruction"? 33
10. When Did God Decide to Give Us
    Eternal Life? 35
11. Isn't Our Heavenly Inheritance Fully
    Guaranteed? 37
12. Aren't Our Good Works Predestined? 39
13. Didn't Jesus Deliberately Hide His
    Message so People Wouldn't Repent? 41
14. Could Judas Have Refused to
    Betray Jesus? 43
15. Don't Evil Men Also Glorify God? 45
16. Can Satan Repent and Be Saved? 47

viii 75 BIBLE QUESTIONS

17. Aren't Men Ordained in Advance
    to Eternal Life? 49
18. Doesn't God Compel Men to Believe
    in Jesus? 51
19. Didn't God Choose Us Long before We
    Accepted Him? 53
20. How Can an Unregenerate Man
    Accept Christ? 55
21. Could the Authorities Have Acted
    Righteously and Released Jesus? 57
22. Isn't God's Grace Irresistible? 59
23. Isn't the Will of God Absolutely Sovereign? ... 61
24. Isn't Faith in Christ the Gift of God? 63
25. Did Christ Die for All Men? 65

Supplement to Part I: Historic Creeds 67
Recommended Reading 83

PART II — Law: God's or Man's 85
Introduction to Part II 87

26. Isn't It Immoral for People to Have
    Sex with Animals? 89
27. How Can We Love God but
    Ignore God's Law? 91
28. Is Profession of Faith Enough, or Do
    Our Acts Also Count? 93
29. If Men Won't Obey God's Law, Are
    They Saved? 95
30. Are We "Once Saved, Always Saved"? 97
31. How Can We Accurately Define Sin if
    We Deny God's Law? 99
32. Does God Answer Prayers of Lawbreakers? ..101
33. Do We Really Love the Brethren if
    We Disobey God's Laws? 103

TABLE OF CONTENTS ix

34. How Can We Identify Christians if We Ignore God's Law? 105
35. How Can We Know if We Are "Dead to Sin" if We Ignore God's Law? 107
36. How Can We "Walk in Newness of Life" if We Disobey God's Law? 109
37. How Can We Stop "Serving Sin" if We Disobey God's Law? 111
38. Since God's Law Can't Kill Us, Won't It Help Us to Live? 113
39. How Can Sin Still "Reign" in Us if We Obey God's Law? 115
40. Aren't Those Who Disobey God's Law "Instruments of Unrighteousness"? 117
41. What Does "Under Grace, Not Law" Mean? ..119
42. Are We Free to Ignore God's Law if We Are "Under Grace"? 121
43. Is a Christian's "New Spirit" Opposed to God's Law? 123
44. Is the Law of God "Carnal" or Holy, Just, and Good? 125
45. How Can We "Walk after the Spirit" if We Disobey God's Law? 127
46. Isn't a "Carnal Mind" One Which Is Opposed to God's Law? 129
47. How Can We "Mortify the Flesh" if We Disobey God's Law? 131
48. Didn't Paul Believe That the Specifics of God's Law Still Apply? 133
49. How Can We Separate the "Moral Law" from God's Laws? 135
50. Doesn't Faith in Christ Establish God's Law? 137

Recommended Reading 139

PART III — Kingdom: God's or Man's 141
Introduction to Part III 143

51. Aren't Those Who Obey God's Law the "Salt of the Earth"? 145
52. Isn't a "City on a Hill" to Be an Example for the World? 147
53. Should We Limit the Areas to Be Illuminated by Our "Light"? 149
54. How Can Christians Be Resurrected before the Millennium? 151
55. Doesn't God's Kingdom Grow Slowly Until It Fills the Earth? 153
56. Doesn't "Leaven" Mean Victory? 155
57. Didn't Christ's Kingdom Begin before the Crucifixion? 157
58. Wasn't Satan Cast out of Heaven During Jesus' Earthly Ministry? 159
59. Isn't Faith Progressively Productive Until Christians Win? 161
60. How Can Satan Rule the World if Power Comes from Righteousness? 163
61. Aren't Christians Supposed to Crush Satan? .. 165
62. What Can Possibly Interrupt Christ's Dominion? 167
63. Isn't Christ's Kingdom in This World? 169
64. Doesn't the New Testament Teach That Christians Are Powerful? 171
65. Aren't Christians Supposed to Execute Judgment? 173
66. Why Shouldn't Christians Become Civil Rulers and Enforce God's Law? 175
67. Doesn't the Bible Require an Appeals Court? 177

TABLE OF CONTENTS xi

68. Won't the Resurrection Take Place after the Millennium?...................179
69. Won't Men Live Longer as God's Kingdom Progresses?................181
70. Doesn't Christ's Kingdom Expand over Time?........................183
71. Doesn't God Want His "Heirs" to Inherit Everything?..................185
72. Didn't the Prophets Foresee the Church Age?.......................187
73. Didn't David Foresee the Church Age?......189
74. Didn't Moses Foresee the Church Age?.....191
75. Aren't There Two Kinds of Salvation?.......193

Recommended Reading 195
Conclusion 199
Appendix A — How to Get Your Answers 205
Appendix B — What Are Biblical Blueprints? 221

Introduction

(it could change your life)

There is a war on, *a war between Christianity and humanism.* Since 1975, hundreds of thousands of Christians in the United States have become aware of the threat to Christianity posed by humanism. It is amazing how long it took for Christians to recognize that humanism is a rival religion: about a century.

Humanism comes in many forms: secular humanism ("man is the measure of all things"), religious humanism ("man is evolving into god"), and even a self-proclaimed Christian humanism ("God's laws and logic and autonomous man's laws and logic really aren't in conflict"). This book deals with the mistakes and outright lies of Christian humanism, since Christian humanism has not yet been seen for what it is by most Bible-believing Christians.

Today, there are tens of thousands of Christian students who attend supposedly Christian colleges. Every day, they are being exposed to the religion of humanism, but always disguised as conservative, fundamentalist, or evangelical Christianity. The Christian student on a secular campus at least recognizes that he is being indoctrinated by representatives of an alien religion; the Christian attending a Christian college or seminary may not recognize this fact. In fact, he probably would be shocked to discover this, and so would the donors to the college.

Back in 1976, I edited a hardback book called *Foundations of Christian Scholarship* which outlines many of the humanist presuppositions that undergird various academic disciplines: psychology, history, education, economics, sociology, mathematics, and philosophy. The book also introduces Christian students to a consistently Christian set of alternatives. The fact is, the presuppositions of *all* the academic disciplines, as taught in secular universities, are hostile to what the Bible teaches about God, man, and law. (You can order a copy of this book from Thoburn Press, P.O. Box 6941, Tyler, TX 75711; $7.50. If you're a college student, you need this book.)

In certain fields, such as psychology, anthropology, and sociology, professors who hold the Ph.D. are virtually always self-conscious humanists and should be regarded by their students as theologically suspect until they can prove their innocence by affirming a biblical view of sin, redemption, and restoration rather than a Freudian or clinical view of sin. Anyone who doubts that Freud was totally incorrect and self-consciously hostile to Christianity from start to finish should read R. J. Rushdoony's short book, *Freud,* published by Presbyterian & Reformed Publishing Co., which also publishes Jay E. Adams' excellent books on counselling, especially *Competent to Counsel.* I would say that any instructor who is forthrightly hostile to Adams' "nouthetic counselling" techniques should also be regarded as guilty until proven innocent. Because psychology is the study of man, the doctrines of sin and redemption are basic for an understanding of psychology. The humanists reject the biblical view of man.

Nevertheless, the sad fact is that many, if not most, of the instructors on Christian campuses share several of the basic philosophical and theological premises of humanism even though they are not self-conscious humanists themselves. They have been taught certain assumptions about the Bible and Christianity that are simply not true, but they really believe that they are true. Even in the Bible departments, these humanist presuppositions have crept in, and the brand of Christianity that emerges is almost helpless in challenging secular humanism, precisely because of their *shared presuppositions* about God, man, and law.

Amazingly, this is even true of some of the most prominent conservative Bible preachers in the nation. I don't mean the less disguised humanism of a Robert Schuller, with his "self-esteem" or "bootstrap" Christian humanism; I mean fundamentalist pastors who have adopted some of the basic principles of humanism, never suspecting that these are the first principles of Christianity's major rival religion.

What this little book provides is 75 simple Bible questions in three subject areas that enable students to test themselves and their instructors to find out if latent humanist presuppositions have compromised their thinking. (I stress the fact that this book is first of all a means of *testing yourself;* Jesus warned us to remove the beam in our own eye before we attempt to remove the splinter from our brother's eye.)

I am not saying that everyone who denies the validity of some or even all of these 75 questions is a humanist. What I *am* saying is that anyone who rejects most of these 75 questions does hold a *compromised* form of Christian doctrine which is incapable of successfully challenging secular humanism. Why? Because of the presuppositions this person shares with the secular humanists.

Readers of this book may be startled to discover that they are already compromised. They may think to themselves, "This can't be true. I'm a Christian, not a humanist. I believe exactly what good Christian teachers have taught me since my youth. They couldn't have been wrong about these matters." Yes, they could have been wrong. In fact, they *were* wrong, which is why for over a century in the United States, conservative, Bible-believing Christians have allowed the secular humanists to take over every area of life: education, psychology, entertainment, business, politics, the arts, communications, the media, and on and on. Because Christians have held to humanist presuppositions in certain key areas, they allowed the secular humanists to take over *by default*.

I want Christians to reconquer this lost territory. I think it's possible, and I think God expects it. I have shown how we can begin to do it in my little paperback book, *Backward, Christian Soldiers?* (Institute for Christian Economics, P.O. Box 8000, Tyler, TX 75711; $5.95). But Christians can't do it if they share humanist presuppositions with the humanists. Third-rate humanists can never defeat first-rate humanists. Christians must purge out all traces of humanism before they can successfully battle humanism.

Why Questions?

There is an old slogan that says "one picture is worth ten thousand words." I have a variation: "One good question is worth fifty assertions." (And 75 good questions are worth . . . ? Let's see . . .)

A well thought-out question opens many possibilities. People who react negatively against an assertion may be willing to think through a good question. If you ask a question properly, it can lead another person to consider a whole new set of ideas. That's why Socrates developed the so-called Socratic method. That's also why Jesus used questions to disarm his opponents, as well as to lead His followers into the kingdom.

When He asked, "What does it profit a man if he should gain the whole world and lose his soul?" He was making a very important spiritual point. His question sticks in the mind in a way that an assertion wouldn't.

That's why this book is a book of questions. They stick in the mind. They enable people to explore new ideas. They don't threaten someone in the way that an outright assertion does. They enable people to think through certain issues, and then *come to their own conclusions.*

This isn't to say that everyone who reads these questions won't feel threatened. On the contrary, some people will feel *extremely* threatened. Not by the questions, but by the answers the Bible gives to these questions. A lot of people who sit down and start to read this book will never get beyond the first three or four questions. In panic or outrage they will toss this book aside and never come back to it.

Why? (A question) Because (here comes an answer) a lot of people have been misinformed about what the Bible teaches. They have come to believe on Jesus Christ as the author of their salvation, which is the proper thing to believe, but they have also come to believe in a lot of other doctrines that Jesus never taught and that the Bible doesn't teach. They have mixed up their commitment to Christ with their commitment to *man-made doctrines* that glorify man rather than Christ. When they begin to think through the implications of just a few of these questions, they run for cover. They say to themselves, "Well, if that's the kind of God this book believes in, I'd rather not believe in Him." *This is why they are compromised!* The important question is: *What kind of God does the Bible really proclaim?* That's the God we're required to believe in. If you read all 75 questions, and think about them, you'll begin to question yourself about the kind of God others have told you that the Bible supposedly proclaims. And once you start rethinking such issues, it's hard to stop, if you're serious about your faith, meaning your faith in God (rather than your faith in what you've been taught in the past).

Maybe you'll wind up temporarily confused. People don't like to be confused. It's painful. But that's what growth is all about—spiritual growth and intellectual growth. That's what it means to become spiritually mature. At some stages of your spiritual life, you're fed milk; at a later stage, you're fed meat. Some of you may not feel that you're ready for meat. You probably won't finish the book. (Question: When *will* you be ready for meat? In a year? In a decade? When you're three score and ten?)

Some of you may be in college or seminary. You're paying big money and spending many hours to chew what you have been told is meat. Maybe it is meat, but maybe it's just leather: tough to chew, but not that nutritional. As long as you're paying to get answers to questions, take advantage of the opportunity. Get these questions answered.

I'm saying that *you've been misinformed* about what the Bible has to say about three things (at the very least): 1) the sovereignty of God, 2) the law of God, and 3) the kingdom of God. Am I overstating my case? There are ways to find out. The first step is to check out everything I say. I've provided a lot of Bible references. Read them. Think about them. Pray about them. Talk about them with other students. See if I'm quoting the Bible erroneously. Remember: it's not what I say, or your instructors say, that matters. *What matters is what the Bible says.*

But maybe after you've read all the Bible verses I cite, you'll still be unconvinced. You'll conclude that those who disagree with me deserve their "day in court." That's what I think right now. That's why I think you should start asking your instructors to give cogent, Bible-based answers to these questions, assuming that they don't agree with the answers I've given (and they won't agree, I can assure you). *Get some answers.* You're paying for them. Then evaluate their answers by the teachings found in the Bible. Go back to the verses I've cited and read them again. Compare my explanations with the answers you received from your instructors. Then make up your own mind. *All I expect is an open hearing.*

Suppressing the Evidence

What I've found over the years is that a lot of Bible instructors object to their opponents getting *their* day in court. These instructors know all about the material in this book, but they don't want their students to know about it. Unless pressed by students, they never even mention that there is a whole different way of looking at the Bible. They would almost rather have students reading *Playboy* than this book, since they have answers (and disciplinary procedures) for students who read *Playboy.* There is one college administration in the South which not only expels any student caught with this book (or materials teaching similar doctrines), it then refuses to send out the student's transcripts. Students can't graduate, and they can't transfer their credits. Theft? Probably. Immoral? Certainly. All done in the name of Jesus? You bet.

(If you now attend such a school, have your transcripts sent out to one or two other colleges immediately, and every semester thereafter, whether you read this book or not. You're vulnerable to the administration's coercion. They are ready and willing to control your conscience by using this threat against you. If necessary, have your transcripts sent out to cooperating business firms that will keep them for you in case you ever get expelled. You can subsequently have these second-party-held transcripts sent to other colleges that know just exactly how perverse certain administrations are, and that will provisionally accept your credits, even though they didn't come directly from your present college's registrar.)

So everyone should get his day in court. You're paying money (or your parents are) to get answers to the big questions in life. This book is designed to help you get biblical answers to legitimate questions. They aren't trick questions. They're Bible questions. You can use them to get answers about:

> Your own state of mind
> Your commitment to getting answers
> Your present knowledge of the Bible
> Your church's commitment to the Bible
> Your teachers' understanding of the Bible
> Your school's commitment to open discussion
> Your readiness to join the fight against humanism

Warning: this book could get you in trouble. You may not want to show it around just yet. It's not designed to get you in trouble, but some people who should be spiritually mature and ready to answer hard questions aren't spiritually mature and aren't ready to answer hard questions. They're ready to put pressure on students who *ask* hard questions. So be discreet. There are many ways to get legitimate questions answered. I've discussed this at length in **Appendix A**. Before you rush in where angels fear to tread, think about the proper strategy in your position. If you're dealing with self-confident, spiritually mature, well-informed instructors, you don't have a problem. If you aren't, you do.

I want to stress the fact that *all I'm asking for is an opportunity to be heard*. I honestly believe that many Bible colleges and churches have been deliberately and unfairly suppressing the information found in this book. On the other hand, I also believe that many others simply haven't been exposed to the arguments I've raised. They are operating out of ignorance. As Paul said of the Hebrews, "they have a zeal of God, but not according to knowledge" (Romans 10:2). They have been well-intentioned in the past, but not according to knowledge.

Honest Discussion

If people are really well-intentioned, they won't object to honest discussion. They may still reject my arguments, but at least they won't resent the fact that you're thinking about these Bible questions. If you conduct yourself graciously, there will be no trouble with well-intentioned instructors. Christian gentlemen will respect the integrity and sincerity of other Christian gentlemen. But if they attack, scream, complain, or threaten you, know for sure that you're not dealing with Christian gentlemen. If they dismiss your questions with some variation of "No Christian could believe such things," or "Those are heretical questions," then they probably don't have any answers. In short, if they refuse to answer legitimate questions, know for sure that *you're dealing with people who are insecure about their own beliefs*. Be gracious at all times, even when they "stonewall" you, but make up your own mind. You're responsible before God for your own mistakes; let them be responsible for theirs.

If your instructors can't give you accurate answers to these 75 questions, or even answers to the half a dozen or so that bother you the most, then you owe it to yourself to keep on studying, reading, thinking, and praying. Just because *they* can't successfully handle these theological issues doesn't mean that nobody can. Follow through on your own. Find others who are willing to get involved with you. Read some of the books I recommend, where you can get answers. Remember: **"But without faith it is impossible to please him: for he that cometh to God must believe that he is, and that he is a rewarder of them that diligently seek him"** (Hebrews 11:6). If you seek Him diligently, you will be rewarded. Don't be like the man described by James: **"For if any be a hearer of the word, and not a doer, he is like unto a man beholding his natural face in a glass [mirror]: For he beholdeth himself, and goeth his way, and straightway forgetteth what manner of man he was"** (James 1:23-24). If you start to ask yourself these questions, but then get scared or lazy and refuse to seek out biblical answers, you are very much like the person James described.

Why I Wrote this Book

I became a Christian in the summer of 1959, just after I had graduated from high school. If I had been given a book like this one to "chew on" before I entered college, I think I would have saved myself a lot of trouble. But no book like this was in print back then.

I met a pastor who was a graduate of Dallas Theological Seminary back in 1961. He provided me with biblical evidence that eventually convinced me of the validity of questions 1-25. He eventually earned a Th.D.

from Dallas. But he himself has never been willing to go on and affirm the validity of questions 26-75. It took me until the spring of 1964, when I was a seminary student, to complete the transformation of my thinking. [Just for the record, I was taking a class on the Book of Romans from Professor John Murray, and his lectures on Romans 11 were what finally swung me over. His arguments are available in his book, *The Epistle to the Romans* (Grand Rapids, Michigan: Eerdmans, 1965). His arguments on Romans 9 are no less eloquent, for those of you who don't agree with questions 1-25.]

I had to learn the hard way. It took me five years after my conversion to figure out what was going on theologically—that I had been misled by most of my Christian teachers and all of the humanist ones. My hope is that this little book will help you, and will speed up your learning process. The book is very simple. The questions are straightforward. There's nothing complicated about them. People may try to make them seem more complicated than they really are. But this, in my view, is a kind of intellectual smoke screen. People who don't like someone else's conclusions have a tendency to say things like, "You're making things too complicated," when in fact the conclusions follow easily from the evidence.

Of course, I could provide lots of complicated evidence, with hundreds of footnotes, but I'm trying to save you time. I'm trying to make things easier for you, not more difficult. This book is nothing more than a very brief introduction, a kind of handbook. You can go on and study the more detailed materials that I list at the end of each section and at the end of the book. But you don't have to. The 75 questions ought to be sufficient.

Before You Begin

I want you to ask yourself a question: "Do I really believe that the Bible is God's absolutely authoritative and inspired word?" If you *can't* honestly answer "yes," then you already accept the number-one presupposition of the humanists. You probably will be repelled and outraged by all 75 questions. But if you do answer in the affirmative, you should be willing to *subordinate your thinking to whatever the Bible plainly teaches*. If you're really willing to do this, then these 75 questions will open up a whole new world to you. Now, are you ready to ask yourself 75 very serious Bible questions? And are you ready to seek out answers if you find that you don't agree with them?

Part I

SOVEREIGNTY: GOD'S OR MAN'S

Introduction to Part I

Who is sovereign over history, man or God? This was Satan's great temptation in the garden: "ye shall be as gods" (Genesis 3:5). Eve decided that she would test God's word by an experiment. She would violate God's law and see whether she would die that very day, as God had promised. She, the "neutral observer," would determine who was correct, God or Satan.

The problem was, by *testing* God's word, she was *violating* God's word. She was setting herself up as the sovereign agent in a cosmic experiment. But God said that He was in charge. He would determine the course of events if she or her husband violated His word. It was clear: either He is sovereign, or He is a liar. Satan tempted men by implying that man is in charge rather than God. By believing that man is in charge of the great cosmic test of God's word, and then acting in terms of this belief, mankind fell into sin.

God's word tests God's word. God's word is the authority, not man's puny attempts to test it. That's where the Christian must start: with the sovereignty of God's revealed word, the Bible. If this isn't his starting point, then he is in sin, pursuing the old sin of Adam and Eve. The man who elevates his supposedly neutral logic or his experimental techniques above the sovereign word of God has committed a gross sin. *We do not test God with our so-called logic; the word of God tests our logic*.

With this in mind, consider the following 25 Bible

questions. They are all concerned with the question: Is God absolutely sovereign over His creation, or is man in any way sovereign? The humanists want to argue that *only* man is sovereign, to the extent that any conscious force is sovereign. As you will see when you read the next 25 questions, the Bible teaches that God, and God alone, is absolutely and comprehensively sovereign. But there are many, many Christians who can't make up their minds between what the Bible teaches and what the humanists teach. They don't want to accept either position.

The Bible doesn't teach a middle position. (That's my assertion.) Are you willing to see what the Bible teaches in this regard? Are you willing to *test my assertion* by asking yourself 25 questions, and then seeking biblical answers?

Question 1
Didn't God Hate the Unborn Infant Esau?

(For the children being not yet born, neither having done any good or evil, that the purpose of God according to election might stand, not of works, but of him that calleth;) It was said unto her, The elder shall serve the younger. As it is written, Jacob have I loved, but Esau have I hated (Romans 9:11-13).

God prophesied to Rebekah the future of her two sons. Esau would serve Jacob. Paul is clear: God pronounced this judgment against Esau, the elder brother, before the two sons were born or had done anything evil.

The text means precisely what it says, which is why it bothers so many Christians. They jump to a false conclusion: "Esau never had a chance to prove himself. Yet it says that God hated him. That's not fair of God. God is fair, so the text couldn't mean what it says. It must mean something else."

Paul knew that this is what people would say, so he immediately asked a rhetorical question which makes sense only if God's hatred of Esau really did begin before Esau had done good or evil: "**What shall we say then? Is there unrighteousness with God? God forbid.**" Paul then goes on to speak of the Pharaoh of the Book of Exodus in similar terms (Question 2).

Paul was quoting Malachi 1:2-4. In verse 3 we read that God even condemned all of Esau's heirs, Edom: "**And I hated Esau, and laid his mountains and his heritage waste. . . .**"

Questionable Answer

"God really didn't condemn Esau before either of the sons was born. He condemned Esau because He foresaw the evil deeds that Esau would do later on. So God isn't unfair. Esau fell by his own evil deeds."

My Reply: But the text is specific: God *did* condemn Esau before he had done anything evil. The text does not mention Esau's future deeds. The point is: *all men are condemned automatically before they are born.* That is what the doctrine of original sin means. Esau was a son of rebellious Adam, just like all the rest of us, and was therefore innately evil and hated by God, just like all the rest of us, before he had done anything moral or immoral. The amazing fact is not that God hated Esau. *The amazing fact is that God loved Jacob!*

Didn't God tell Rebekah that the elder would serve the younger? Could Esau have lived a good life and have reversed that promise? Isaac thought so, and he was ready to give the blessing to Esau (Genesis 27:4). But Isaac was wrong; God made it possible for Jacob to receive the blessing despite his father's act of rebellion (Genesis 27:6-29).

Was Esau helpless? Yes. Was it inevitable that Jacob get the blessing? That is what God told Rebekah (Genesis 25:23). Could she rely on God's promise? Absolutely. Did Esau have a chance of overcoming God's promise? Not a chance. Question: *Is there any meaning to the word "chance" in God's plan?*

For further study: Ps. 5:5; 11:5; Rom. 11:7-10; Eph. 2:3; Heb. 12:16-17.

Question 2
Could Pharaoh Have Repented?

For the scripture saith unto Pharaoh, Even for this same purpose have I raised thee up, that I might shew my power in thee, and that my name might be declared throughout all the earth (Romans 9:17).

Did God raise up Pharaoh for the wrong purpose? Or was magnifying His own glory a sufficient purpose for raising up Pharaoh? But if He raised up Pharaoh for this purpose, then how could Pharaoh have overcome God's purpose by repenting and allowing the Hebrews to depart Egypt in peace?

Before Moses began his mission to the people of Israel, God promised that He would harden Pharaoh's heart. **"And I will harden Pharaoh's heart, and multiply my signs and my wonders in the land of Egypt. But Pharaoh shall not hearken unto you, that I may lay my hand upon Egypt . . ."** (Exodus 7:3-4a).

God actively hardened Pharaoh's heart, *in order that* He might "lay His hand upon"—judge—Egypt. This is what He told Moses about His plan well in advance of Moses' first confrontation with Pharaoh. Could Pharaoh have overcome God's hardening of his heart? How? **"The king's heart is in the hand of the LORD, as the rivers of water: he turneth it whithersoever he will"** (Proverbs 21:1). Result: **"And the LORD hardened the heart of Pharaoh, and he hearkened not unto them; as the LORD had spoken unto Moses"** (Exodus 9:12). The Bible is clear: *Pharaoh was under the sovereign control of God.*

Questionable Answer

"But the Bible says that Pharaoh hardened his own heart (Exodus 8:15, 32). We are not to blame God for this hardening of Pharaoh's heart. Pharaoh was exercising his own free will. God judged him for his own sins."

My Reply: The Bible unquestionably says that Pharaoh hardened his own heart. He was a *responsible moral agent*. But this does not answer the initial question, namely, could Pharaoh have repented? Could he have softened his heart, despite God?

> **And the LORD said unto Moses, Go in unto Pharaoh: for I have hardened his heart, and the heart of his servants, that I might shew these my signs before him: And that thou mayest tell in the ears of thy son, and of thy son's son, what things I have wrought in Egypt, and my signs which I have done among them; that ye may know how that I am the LORD (Exodus 10:1-2).**

If Pharaoh had repented of his sins, and had turned the Hebrews free, how could God's word have been fulfilled? Can we ever say that the will of sinful man (or even righteous man) can prevail against the declared intent of God?

And if He did this to Pharaoh, why not to other rebels?

For further study: Ex. 4:21; 7:13, 22; 9:12, 35; 14:8; Isa. 6:10; 63:17.

Question 3
Does God's Absolute Predestination Make Him Unfair?

Thou wilt say then unto me, Why doth he yet find fault? For who hath resisted his will? (Romans 9:19).

Paul was a logician. He knew exactly what confused (or rebellious) men would ask themselves, once he had described the hardening of Pharaoh's heart by God. The person who was unwilling to accept the truth of Paul's words would reply: "You are saying that God didn't give Pharaoh a fair shake. Pharaoh might have repented. But God didn't allow him to repent. What kind of God is that? You say He is omnipotent. Then He isn't fair. Who could resist the will of an omnipotent God? But such a God is not a God of ethics, for He restricts men's ethical behavior. I don't believe in your God. In other words, Paul, you have misrepresented God. You have borne false witness against Him. God is either righteous or else He is sovereign—a predestinating God. But He cannot be both. I prefer to believe in a righteous God who grants men autonomous free will. Better a world of chance than a predestined world."

Paul's response to such logic is offensive to autonomous men: **"Nay but, O man, who art thou that repliest against God? Shall the thing formed say to him that formed it, Why hast thou made me thus? Hath not the potter power over the clay, of the same lump to make one vessel unto honour, and another unto dishonour?"** (vv. 20-21). In short, *be silent, complainer!* God is sovereign. Do not raise a logical paradox: "righteousness vs. omnipotence."

Questionable Answer

"The sovereignty of God really doesn't mean predestination. It means that God is powerful, but in His mercy, He allows men an area of free choice, so that in no way is God the author of sin. Men are given free will and free choice. He is fair because He voluntarily limits His own total power."

My Reply: Then what is the meaning of the phrase, **"vessels of wrath fitted to destruction"** (v. 22)? What is a vessel made by a potter *unto*—for the purpose of—destruction? If it is not made for a purpose, is it random? But Paul spoke of two sorts of vessels, with both kinds *made* for respective purposes. Listen to Isaiah's warning to those theologians who place the sovereignty of God in opposition to the fairness of God:

> **Woe unto him that striveth with his Maker! Let the potsherd strive with the potsherds of the earth. Shall the clay say to him that fashioneth it, What makest thou . . . ?** (Isaiah 45:9).

Some questions should not be asked. One of them is this one: "If God is omnipotent, how can He be fair in judging men for their sins?" Another is: "If man is morally responsible, how can God predestinate all events?" Paul's answer: *"Be silent!"*

Test your commitment to the Bible. Are you trying to judge the truth of the Bible by your own logic? Are you disobeying Paul?

For further study: Job 9:12-15; 33:12-13; Isa. 29:16.

Question 4

If We Can't Work Our Way INTO Salvation, How Can We Work Our Way OUT?

For he saith to Moses, I will have mercy on whom I will have mercy, and I will have compassion on whom I will have compassion. So then it is not of him that willeth, nor of him that runneth, but of God that sheweth mercy (Romans 9:15-16).

We cannot work our way into salvation. This is the doctrine of grace. But the question needs to be raised: Can we work our way *out* of salvation?

If God says that he will have compassion on someone, how can that person escape God's compassion? How can the will of God be thwarted by rebellious man? If we say that rebellious man can reject God's compassion, aren't we saying that rebellious man can defeat the plan and providence of God?

The context of Paul's words is familiar by now: the question of God's hatred. Esau was hated by God before he was born. Pharaoh was destroyed by God in order to demonstrate God's power. So Paul's readers may ask: **"Is there unrighteousness with God?"** (Romans 9:14). Paul's reply: **"God Forbid."** God can vent His wrath on anyone He chooses to destroy, and the person who is a vessel unto dishonor can't do a thing about it.

With this as his basic argument, Paul then shifts his focus. God's mercy is as irresistible as His wrath. Even as the objects of His wrath cannot escape, so the objects of His compassion cannot escape. What else could his argument mean?

Questionable Answer

"But Paul really wasn't arguing that the wrath of God is inescapable, so therefore he could not have meant that the mercy of God is inescapable. Men have the free choice: to continue to be objects of his wrath or not. The vessel of wrath and the vessel of honor can switch places. It's a question of human choice, not God's foreordained decision."

My Reply: What does the text say? It says that God hated Esau before Esau had done good or evil. It also says that He loved Jacob, before Jacob had done good or evil. They were not yet born, yet God had already made His decision as to which was a vessel of honor and which was a vessel of dishonor. And from that decision God never wavered.

What about Pharaoh? Paul tells us precisely what Pharaoh was: an object of dishonor. Pharaoh could not become a vessel of honor, any more than Moses could become a vessel of dishonor. God showed mercy to Jacob and Moses. They could not escape. God's will is irresistible.

It is the force of Paul's words regarding the vessels of dishonor which undergirds his words concerning vessels of honor. Those who are vessels of honor are as *safe* as those who are vessels of dishonor are *doomed*. It is not our willing or our running that establishes either condition. God's decision does.

Do you understand now why you never hear sermons on Romans 9?

For further study: Ps. 115:3; Isa. 14:27; Ezek. 37:1-14; Dan. 4:35; Acts 13:48; Eph. 2:4-6.

Question 5
How Can God GUARANTEE Good for His People without PREDESTINATING Good?

And we know that all things work together for good to them that love God, to them who are the called according to his purpose (Romans 8:28).

All things? Does this mean each and every thing? That's what the text says.

Consider the implications of this promise. It means that the whole of a regenerate person's life is under the guarantee of God. Each act, each decision has meaning. Even evil acts have a part to play—a part that works together with all other parts. The whole is assured; therefore, the parts must be equally assured. But if the parts are assured, in advance, to fit together in a whole, doesn't this mean predestination? How else could God guarantee the outcome of "all things"? What does the next verse say?

For whom he did foreknow, he also did predestinate to be conformed to the image of his Son, that he might be the firstborn among many brethren.

Could Christ have become the firstborn among *few* brethren? Among *no* brethren? God says no. Christ was the firstborn among *many brethren*. God has *predestinated* their presence, in time and in eternity. Can any man—even the individual whose conversion has been predestined—void God's guarantee? How?

Questionable Answer

"When God says 'predestinates,' He really means 'foreknowledge.' God knows in advance who will accept or reject him (or accept His grace, and then later fall from grace), and He guarantees the *potential* for all things working together for good. But He does not guarantee actual good. He only foreknows the potential for good."

My Reply: The text is clear. All things work together for good. Not some—*all*. Unless usage says otherwise, we have to take the word seriously.

Then Paul raises the issue of predestination. This follows his discussion of "all things." How much plainer could he be? God guarantees all things because He predestinates all things to benefit His followers. Yes, Paul says that God "foreknew" His followers, but then he says that God predestinates. What does predestinate mean? Doesn't Paul say that it means the guaranteeing of all things (events) to fit into the overall plan of God? His guarantee makes sense only within the framework of His sovereign power to bring all things to pass in a way that produces good for those called according to His *purpose.*

Foreknowledge and predestination go together, Paul says. You can't have one without the other. Can anyone show how the biblical definition of foreknowledge negates predestination?

If "predestination" means "foreknowledge," why does Paul use both words in the same sentence?

For further study: Dan. 2:20-21; 5:25-31; Matt. 11:27; 20:15; 22:14; Luke 10:22.

Question 6
How Can We Escape the Love of God?

Moreover whom he did predestinate, them he also called: and whom he called, them he also justified: and whom he justified, them he also glorified. What shall we then say to these things? If God be for us, who can be against us? *(Romans 8:30-31).*

The order of salvation is clear enough. Once God designates a person for eternal blessings, there is no escape. There is *no escape out of wrath* for those who aren't predestinated, called, justified, and glorified. There is *no escape out of blessing* for those who are. This is Paul's doctrine of election.

This passage is God's assurance of victory to His people. What more glorious cry is there anywhere than **"If God be for us, who can be against us?"** Will Satan defeat God? Can he conceivably defeat God? If Satan is said to have a possibility of beating God in *particulars*, then there is no way for God to accurately guarantee His followers of victory *overall*. The whole, after all, is made up of the parts. If Satan can snatch *one* of God's chosen people out of the pathway to eternal life, then he can conceivably snatch them *all* out. Then Christ is left by Himself, the firstborn, potentially, of *no brethren*. But this is precisely what Paul *denies* in Romans 8:29! How can Satan overcome the decision of God to regenerate someone?

But then the contrary must be true: *since God guarantees the overall victory, He also guarantees the **individual** victories.*

Questionable Answer

"God limits the potentiality of Satan's victories in individual cases. Satan is allowed to be successful in separating *some* of God's chosen people from God's love, but not everyone. Of course, God could have guaranteed that all regenerate men persevere to the end, but he leaves the possibility open for some to perish."

My Reply: The text is clear. Paul specifically argues that there is no power on earth or in heaven that can successfully challenge God's electing grace. What else do these verses mean? What sense can be made out of them if they don't mean this?

If God opens the possibility for some men to fall from grace, then can He guarantee that all the others are safe? Is His predestinating grace assured for at least *some* people? Does anyone want to argue that God picks the raw number of His elect who cannot fall from grace, but not the actual people? Then how can God affirm that all things work for good to those specific people who are called according to His purpose? All things work together for good in *which people's lives?* If He doesn't determine which people are elect, how can He guarantee the *specific details* of the *total blessing* to *all* His chosen people? Does God affirm His love to mere numbers of *indeterminate* people, but not *specific* people? God loves numbers?

If Satan can separate *one* person from God's grace, why can't he separate *everyone*? Does *autonomous man* decide?

For further study: John 6:37-39; 13:18; 15:16, 19; 17:2, 6, 9.

Question 7
If We Can "Fall from Grace," Isn't Christ's Intercession Ineffective?

> Who shall lay any thing to the charge of God's elect? It is God that justifieth. Who is he that condemneth? It is Christ that died, yea rather, that is risen again, who is even at the right hand of God, who also maketh intercession for us (Romans 8:33-34).

The word "elect" means chosen of God. If God makes this choice, can Satan negate it, by working through a rebellious heart? How? How can an elect person have a rebellious heart after he is saved by God's grace? Isn't the very idea of regeneration based on the changing of a person's heart by God?

Once a person is elect, can Satan make a successful accusation against him—an accusation that will persuade God to hand over the person to Satan? If we argue this way, aren't we arguing that Christ's death and resurrection are not all-powerful? Is there some missing bit of power or authority in Christ's death and resurrection?

Furthermore, Paul says that *Christ makes intercession before God the Father on our behalf*. Is being at the right hand of God not an affirmation of His total power—the power He said He possessed after His resurrection (Matthew 28:18)? If Christ is making intercession for His elect, are His prayers and arguments questionable? Is there some likelihood that God will not listen to His Son, and not respond as Christ asks? *Doesn't God the Father trust the judgment of His Son?* Think about it.

Questionable Answer

"The meaning of 'elect' is not what you think. To be elect means that you have only a *chance* for eternal life after Christ regenerates you. Nothing is certain, however. When God says 'Who is he that condemneth?' He doesn't mean that a regenerate man can't decide to become unregenerate and thereby condemn himself. Regenerate man always has the option of condemning himself by sinning."

My Reply: In other words, *I* am powerful enough to condemn myself, even though Christ makes intercession for me to God the Father. My power is so great that I can overcome the election of God and the intercession of Christ. God grants me this power, of course, but I do possess it. And therefore Satan can tempt me the same way he tempted Adam and Eve. He can appeal to my autonomy—my God-granted limited autonomy—in order to get me to condemn myself. He can thereby snatch me away from the electing power of God. Christ's intercession fails again.

Why does God not honor the prayers of His Son? Are Christ's prayers half-way prayers? Aren't they meaningful, honest prayers to preserve His elect from disgrace? If Satan has the power to reverse God's very election of His people, in the face of Christ's intercessory prayer, *then what confidence can Christians have in their own prayers?* Are God's answers to prayers *random*? If autonomous man can overcome Christ's prayers, then hasn't Satan defeated Christ? Hasn't Satan destroyed the power of prayer?

For further study: John 10:28-30; Rom. 11:2, 5-7; II Thess. 2:13.

Question 8
Are We LESS than Conquerors?

Who shall separate us from the love of Christ? Shall tribulation, or distress, or persecution, or famine, or nakedness, or peril, or sword? As it is written, For thy sake we are killed all the day long; we are accounted as sheep for the slaughter. Nay, in all these things we are more than conquerors through him that loved us (Romans 8:35-37).

Can we fall from grace? We will no doubt be tempted: by tribulation, distress, persecution, famine, nakedness, peril, or sword. You can understand why Paul wrote this passage to the church in Rome. But what is his answer to the question? *No!* In all these things we are more than conquerors.

Here it is again: *all these things*. Again, do all things work together for good to them who are called according to God's purpose? Yes, they *certainly* do. But how can God guarantee this? How can He guarantee this victory, if He has reserved to man and Satan areas of *potential* rebellion by which His elect can become ethical rebels, cursed of God? After all, the potential can become actual. This is what "potential" means.

Is going to hell what God means when He promises His people good? A most peculiar meaning of "good"! But if they cannot go to hell, then they are truly elect, truly guaranteed the victory. They can be persecuted, but not separated from God's love. If God's elect can perish, then where is God's victory?

Questionable Answer

"Actually, Paul's question is not what it looks like. It looks rhetorical, but it isn't. He only sounds as though he is saying that nothing can separate us from the love of God. In fact, *we* can separate ourselves from God's love. Besides, the "us" he refers to are indeterminate people, though perhaps a determinate *number* of people. After we die, *then* nobody can separate us—those of us who never actually get separated before we die—from the love of God."

My Reply: How can anyone be threatened *after* death by tribulation, distress, persecution, and so forth? Of course dead Christians are safe then from being separated from God's love by these threats. They aren't threats any longer. But Paul is talking about not being separated from God's love during life on earth, when these threats are real. So who are the "us" on earth he refers to?

Doesn't "us" refer to all regenerate people, all of whom are protected from separation from God's love *before* they die physically? Who among "us" can fall? If this isn't what "us" means, why does Paul mention all those trials and tribulations?

Also, why does he use what is obviously a rhetorical argument—"Who can separate us from the love of God?"—if he really believes that someone can? How could a master of biblical logic misuse words this way? How can an elect person fall from grace?

For further study: Jer. 32:40; John 5:24; 10:27; Phil. 1:6; I Thess. 5:9, 23-24; II Thess. 3:3; I Pet. 1:4-5, 9.

Question 9
Doesn't God Make "Vessels Fitted For Destruction"?

What if God, willing to shew his wrath, and to make his power known, endured with much longsuffering the vessels of wrath fitted to destruction: And that he might make known the riches of his glory on the vessels of mercy, which he had afore prepared unto glory . . . ? (Romans 9:22-23).

Paul contrasts two kinds of vessels: some fitted for destruction and some fitted for mercy. He uses a similar contrast in verse 21: vessels unto honor and vessels unto dishonor. He also describes God as a potter, a maker of vessels. But vessels are designed by their maker. They are assigned a purpose by their maker. Does this mean that God actually designed people as vessels to be filled with His wrath?

We know that the vessels of mercy were **"afore prepared unto glory."** He endures vessels of wrath, Paul says, not in order to save them, but in order to display His glory to vessels of mercy. Vessels of wrath therefore have a purpose in God's plan of salvation. He prepared one kind of vessel before time began: vessels of mercy. What about the other kind?

Can we discuss God, the creator of vessels of mercy, without discussing God, the creator of vessels of wrath? Paul discusses both. He indicates that one type (wrath) exists only to demonstrate God's mercy to the other type. If He predestinates some men to salvation, how can the others escape wrath?

Questionable Answer

"Paul's use of the words 'potter' and 'vessel' are figurative. He did not really mean to convey the idea of a master craftsman molding living vessels. Thus, Paul did not mean that God actually designed certain specific 'vessels,' meaning people, either to receive His mercy or His wrath. A vessel is simply a type, a design; men decide which type they wish to become. God offers each person this choice."

My Reply: Yes, Paul's use of the words "potter" and "vessel" are figurative, symbolic—figures of speech. But what, exactly, are these figures supposed to convey to us theologically? We know that God is the Creator. Doesn't that point to the analogy of the potter? And if the analogy of the potter is proper, then shouldn't we regard ourselves and all people as vessels? And if we are vessels, aren't we *designed* vessels? Doesn't each of us have a role to play in God's cosmic drama? Satan does; why not equally specific men? Satan and specific rebellious angels are specific beings for whom hell was specifically designed (Matthew 25:41). Why not specific rebellious men, too?

God doesn't send "designs" to hell; He sends specific people to hell. Paul says that God designed His chosen people to be vessels of mercy, and that He endures vessels of wrath (such as Pharaoh) in order to demonstrate His power. Was Paul wrong? If he was wrong, then what *is* a vessel of wrath fitted for destruction? A potentially empty concept?

For further study: Gen. 15:16; Isa. 10:5-15.

Question 10
When Did God Decide to Give Us Eternal Life?

According as he hath chosen us in him before the foundation of the world, that we should be holy and without blame before him in love: Having predestinated us unto the adoption of children by Jesus Christ to himself, according to the good pleasure of his will (Ephesians 1:4-5).

"**Before the foundation of the world**" God actively *chose* us. He had a purpose: that we should be holy and without blame before Him.

What about adoption? Did God adopt us because we had already become holy and without blame? Obviously not. Then why did He adopt us at all? In order to conform us to His will. Then why doesn't He adopt everyone? Why leave anyone outside the family of God? We can only answer, "Because He chose to."

All men are created. Adam was God's created son; so are all men. But Adam rebelled. He was cast out of the garden by God—*disinherited*. God must adopt sons if any are to be saved. He transforms them *ethically*. But when does He decide to do this? Immediately after a person repents? Paul says that we were predestinated for adoption before the foundation of the world. We were predestined, meaning *destined before*. And what was our destination? First, an ethical condition: ethical conformity to God. Second, a place: heaven, and then the reconstructed earth. If God established our destination before the foundation of the world, how can any man tell God "I'm not going"?

Questionable Answer

"What Paul means is that as a whole unit, the church was predestined to adoption. God set up His adoption agency before time began. But as to who gets adopted, that is decided by the orphans. God predestined the *whole church;* he did *not* predestine *individual church members.*"

My Reply: Quite frankly, how was God so sure that anyone would accept His offer of adoption? Pharaoh didn't. Judas didn't. Hitler and Stalin didn't. If Saul of Tarsus had had his way, there would never have been an Apostle Paul. So how did God predestinate the church to adoption without predestinating certain individual members? How does God guarantee the future existence of the whole without guaranteeing the future existence of the parts?

Was Jacob adopted? Obviously. When? Before the foundation of the world. Was he adopted because of his fine qualities? No; he was adopted before he was born. Paul makes all of this inescapably clear in Romans 9.

But what about Esau? Was he adopted? Obviously not. Why not? Why couldn't he have signed up to accept God's universal offer of adoption? Because God chose not to adopt him. Without God's personal selection of a person—His declaration that "This person is my adopted child"—there is no adoption. But once this declaration is made, how can man "unadopt" himself?

For further study: Ps. 33:11; Isa. 46:10; Matt. 25:34; Rom. 9:11-16; II Tim. 1:9; Rev. 17:8.

Question 11
Isn't Our Heavenly Inheritance Fully Guaranteed?

In whom also we have obtained an inheritance, being predestinated according to the purpose of him who worketh all things after the counsel of his own will (Ephesians 1:11).

Who is "we"? Paul was writing to someone. He said that **"we have obtained an inheritance."** He included himself among that select group. Therefore, it must have been a group made up of *specific individuals*, namely, Christians who believed Paul's message concerning God's salvation of His people.

He says explicitly, **"we *have* obtained an inheritance."** The inheritance has already been set aside. True, God has not delivered it. He has made a *down payment* on it, however. In Paul's language, God has offered us an *earnest*. He says to the readers to whom he was writing, **"ye were sealed with that holy Spirit of promise, which is the earnest of our inheritance until the redemption of the purchased possession, unto the praise of his glory"** (vv. 13b, 14).

Does the Holy Spirit of *promise* lie to us? Does he offer us (including Paul) a down payment on spiritual blessings that He may not be able to deliver, because "we" later depart from the family into which we have been adopted? Can we trust Him or not? If not, why does Paul call Him the Spirit of promise? Why not "the Spirit of Possibilities"? Is God's promise a "maybe"? Is the Holy Spirit a "Spirit of Maybe"?

37

Questionable Answer

"The text speaks of 'an inheritance, being predestined,' but this only means that the predestined inheritance will never be removed as a *possibility* for men to attain through faith in Christ. It will always be there *in general*, but it is *not* predestined to be there for each *specific* person who may at one point in time become regenerate. He can fall from grace, and thereby lose his inheritance."

My Reply: A down payment is a promise. To whom is it a promise? To "us," Paul says. This clearly means the members of Christ's spiritual body, the invisible church.

If God gives a person a spiritual down payment—a guarantee of future payment to an adopted son—how can He ever cancel the promise? If the promise is conditional on man's part, then in what sense is the inheritance predestined? How can God or man be certain that on their death beds, all Christians will not repent away from God and renounce their status as adopted children of God? If men can fall from grace, why couldn't this take place? In short, what *guarantees* that it won't? The heart of man? How reliable is the heart of man (Jeremiah 17:9)?

Does God waste the down payment on the predestined inheritance on people who will renounce His presentation of sonship? Isn't His adoption of His people equally as secure as it is predestined?

If this isn't the meaning of adoption, what does "predestination" mean?

For further study: Prov. 28:26; Jas. 2:5; I Pet. 1:4.

Question 12
Aren't Our Good Works Predestined?

For we are his workmanship, created in Christ Jesus unto good works, which God hath before ordained that we should walk in them (Ephesians 2:10).

These words are less well known than those that immediately precede them: **"For by grace are ye saved through faith; and that not of yourselves: it is the gift of God: Not of works, lest any man should boast"** (2:8-9). The order of salvation is set forth: 1) by God's grace; 2) through faith; 3) unto predestined good works.

The words **"before ordained"** are crucial. Ordained by whom? By God. When? Before. Again, we find that Paul's letter to the Ephesian church focuses on what God has done *before time began*. His word is sure, and their salvation is sure.

God does not simply predestine a man's moment of salvation, in time and on earth. He also predestines a man's lifelong response to that salvation: his good works. Since men are rewarded in terms of their works (I Corinthians 3), God establishes men's inheritance before the foundation of the world. They will work out on earth their assigned roles, according to the decree of God.

If this is an incorrect interpretation, then what is it that God ordains beforehand? Bare possibilities? Could we be saved by grace through faith, and then do nothing but bad works? We would not then be Christians (I John 1:3-6).

Questionable Answer

"What God ordains is a lifetime of good works that Christians have the *possibility* of performing. He establishes beforehand the *possibilities in general* but it is up to men to make them into *specific actualities*."

My Reply: Paul returns to his theme of God as the master craftsman. **"We are his workmanship."** Poor workmanship? Broken vessels? Unreliable performers? A discredit to His name? People who will take on the name of God as adopted members of His family, and then go out and sin continually?

On what basis can God be confident that His people will walk in the good works that He ordained beforehand, if He cannot (or will not) see to it that what He has ordained comes to pass, case by individual case? What good is the bare possibility of performance in a world which is essentially uncontrolled by God and random as to the outcome of events? What good are God's pre-ordained *general possibilities* in a world governed by the hearts and minds of *specific individuals*—especially individuals who can fall from grace, if they refuse to honor God's "pre-ordained possibilities" for doing good works?

Do all things work together for good to them who are called according to His purpose (Romans 8:28)? Isn't this promise possible because God has already ordained our good works?

Is God totally dependent on our autonomous good works in order to make all things work together for good? How would a humanist answer this question?

For further study: I Cor. 12:3; Col. 3:12; I Pet. 1:2; II Pet. 1:3-10.

Question 13
Didn't Jesus Deliberately Hide His Message so People Wouldn't Repent?

And the disciples came, and said unto him, Why speakest thou unto them in parables? He answered and said unto them, Because it is given unto you to know the mysteries of the kingdom of heaven, but to them it is not given (Matthew 13:10, 11).

The disciples did not always understand Jesus' parables. They had to come to Him for an explanation. They asked Him about this, for if *they* needed an explanation, how much more did the masses who gathered to hear Him only occasionally need an explanation? Why didn't He speak more plainly?

If His goal was to communicate His message clearly, and to a large audience, then the disciples had a good point. They must have assumed that Jesus did want to communicate to a broad audience. Jesus told them that, quite the contrary, His message was not for the masses of Hebrews who came to hear Him. His was an *elitist message*, at least at that stage of His ministry:

For whosoever hath, to him shall be given, and he shall have more abundance: but whosoever hath not, from him shall be taken away even that [which] he hath (Matthew 13:12).

But weren't these people in need of the clear message of salvation? Certainly, just as Judas and Pharaoh were in need. Need is not what determines man's response to the gospel.

Questionable Answer

"Jesus knew that these people were not ready for a complete version of His message. They had to be spoon-fed. He did intend eventually to present a clear version of His spiritual truths, but His ministry was cut short by the crucifixion. His intention was to introduce all people to the mysteries of the faith."

My Reply: What Jesus said was not that He intended to give them a better picture of the gospel later on. What He said was that the multitudes had not been given the opportunity to know the mysteries of the kingdom. He said nothing about speaking to them more clearly later on. On the contrary, He specifically said that *He intended that they should perish:*

For this people's heart is waxed gross, and their ears are dull of hearing, and their eyes they have closed; lest at any time they should see with their eyes, and hear with their ears, and should understand with their heart, and should be converted, and I should heal them (v. 15).

Does this mean that Jesus did His best to keep these people from repenting, to hide the mysteries of the gospel from them? If it doesn't mean this, what else could it mean?

And more to the point, why *did* Jesus speak in parables that even the disciples couldn't understand?

For further study: Matt. 11:25-27; Mark 4:11-12; Luke 8:10; 10:21-22; John 12:39-40.

Question 14
Could Judas Have Refused to Betray Jesus?

But, behold, the hand of him that betrayeth me is with me on the table. And truly the Son of man goeth, as it was determined: but woe unto that man by whom he is betrayed! (Luke 22:21-22).

Judas had a part to play in God's cosmic drama, just as Pharaoh did. The text is specific: 1) there was no other way for Jesus to have died, except by betrayal; and 2) woe unto the man whose act of betrayal was long before determined.

It is obvious that the crucifixion was in God's decree before the foundation of the world. On what other basis could God have chosen to redeem those sinners whom he had predestinated to adoption (Ephesians 1:4-5)? The crucifixion was not a random event. It had to take place. It was only on the basis of the crucifixion that mankind after Adam's rebellion was enabled by God to exist. Without the crucifixion, on the day Adam ate of the fruit, he would have died physically as well as spiritually.

If man has free will, why was this act of Judas inevitable? Why couldn't he have decided not to betray Jesus? Because the crucifixion was predestined. *Someone* had to betray Jesus. Someone had to sin against God in this way. Woe unto the man by whom Christ was betrayed, yet someone must do it, Jesus announced. Jesus knew who it would be. It was not going to be one of the other disciples. Judas will be held responsible throughout eternity, yet there was no escape. Christ had to die as planned.

Questionable Answer

"Yes, Jesus had to die. He said that He had to be betrayed. He knew Judas would do it. But it could have been someone else. It didn't have to be Judas. It was Judas' decision, and he is fully responsible. He was not determined by God to do the deed."

My Reply: If Jesus had to die by betrayal, then someone had to do it. Someone would have to bear the consequences of this supreme act of rebellion. It was Judas. *Inescapable* woe unto him.

Why Judas? Because God had so determined. Judas was determined, and not by impersonal fate. Judas was a sinner, a thief (John 12:6). He was determined—self-determined, yes, but determined also by the decree of God—to pursue his evil plan.

Someone had to do it. Someone had to suffer the consequences. Why Judas? Why *not* Judas? God's plan is not indeterminate. It wasn't that one person *in general* had to do it; it was that one person *in particular* had to do it. Acts of rebellion are performed by persons. They are not empty boxes that are left open for anyone in general to wander into. Predestination isn't performed in a personal vacuum. There is nothing in the Bible that says: "God has determined that a particular event will take place, but it is completely random as to who will perform the deed." Any given event is part of a determined mosaic: *each part fits.*

If each event in history were not predestined, God's plan would not be whole. History would become random.

For further study: Matt. 18:7; 26:24; Mark 14:21.

Question 15
Don't Evil Men Also Glorify God?

The LORD hath made all things for himself: yea, even the wicked for the day of evil (Proverbs 16:4).

The Psalmist announced: **"All thy works shall praise thee, O LORD"** (145:10a). The whole creation testifies to His power and majesty. God does not tempt men to do evil; their own lusts tempt them (James 1:13-14). But these acts do not reduce the glory of God. God makes evil men for Himself, not to save them, but to demonstrate His sovereign power over them and their sin. Like Pharaoh, evil men are judged, and when they are judged, God's name is glorified.

Did God make evil men? Of course; God is the creator. Did God make men evil? No; he hates evil. Did He make evil men in terms of His unshakable and totally inescapable decree? How else? Did He make them randomly? Are they evil only by chance—impersonal chance, which God does not control and may not fully comprehend? (Some Protestant theologians actually say that God does not fully know the future, and that His ignorance is the basis of man's free will and moral responsibility.)

The day of evil for the wicked is the day of final judgment. God made them for this day, just as he made Satan: **"Then shall he say also unto them on the left hand, Depart from me, ye cursed, into everlasting fire, prepared for the devil and his angels"** (Matthew 25:41). The fire was actually designed for them. Weren't they, as vessels of wrath, also designed for it?

Questionable Answer

"God does receive glory from His punishment of all sin, and even sinners. Nevertheless, God is not the author of sin. To say that God makes evil men for His own purposes is the same as saying that God is the author of sin. The text means only that God is glorified *despite* evil men."

My Reply: Is this what the text says? Doesn't it say that God is the Creator who makes *all things* for Himself? Does it imply that sin is the result of a "cosmic accident," over which God had no control, or chose not to exercise any control—an event that thwarted His plan for the ages? Was Satan successful in thwarting God's plan? Or shall we argue that God has no comprehensive plan for the ages? And if we argue this way, what explicit Bible references will we appeal to in order to prove our point?

Are we using human logic—"God is not the author of sin, and therefore sin was never a part of God's plan"—in order to reject what the text says? Are we using human logic—"sin could not be part of the plan of God unless God is the author of sin"—to demonstrate that Satan and his followers autonomously overcame God's hopes and plan for the ages? Have we elevated Satan to a position of "almost God" in power—a being who can, has, and may continue to thwart God's plan? Are we hiding in logic from the teaching of the Bible? Can we trust anti-revelational logic?

For further study: Gen. 45:8; 50:20; Jud. 14:4; Ps. 76:10; Isa. 45:7; Amos 3:6; Acts 3:18; Rom. 8:28; 11:36.

Question 16
Can Satan Repent and Be Saved?

Then shall he say also unto them on the left hand, Depart from me, ye cursed, into everlasting fire, prepared for the devil and his angels (Matthew 25:41).

Is it possible that demons condemned to hell will ever receive eternal life? No. The contents of hell will be dumped into the lake of fire on the day of judgment. **"And death and hell were cast into the lake of fire. This is the second death. And whosoever was not found written in the book of life was cast into the lake of fire"** (Revelation 20:14-15).

If hell was *long ago* prepared to hold Satan and his angels, then how can they escape? It would be like saying that God's kingdom is equally uncertain, even though it, too, was prepared by God: **"Then shall the King say unto them on his right hand, Come, ye blessed of my Father, inherit the kingdom prepared for you from the foundation of the world"** (Matthew 25:34). Each place was prepared by God for *specific* creatures.

Isn't Satan a living creature? Can't he feel pain? Isn't hell an eternal horror for Satan and his demonic angels? Why does God condemn them inescapably to eternal torment? If we acknowledge that Satan's doom is absolutely sure, then we are saying that *Satan has no "chance" of being saved*. And if we admit that he and his angelic followers are *inescapably doomed*, why is it so shocking to say that his *human* followers are equally inescapably doomed? Is God being unfair to Satan and his followers?

Questionable Answer

"Satan and his followers are already in hell. While humans live, they can escape this judgment. Satan can no more escape judgment today than a sinner will be able to after he dies."

My Reply: All this is true, but totally irrelevant. The question is: *Could Satan have repented **after** his rebellion?* Man is given an opportunity to repent after *his* rebellion, but what about Satan? The Bible never even hints at such a possibility. Is God unjust, therefore, in refusing to give Satan a "chance" after his rebellion? Have you ever heard a Christian say so?

God offers the gospel to fallen humans, but apart from their *prior* regeneration, they cannot respond in faith (Question 19). So what is the difference in *effect*? An offer of salvation *which cannot be received by any rebellious person whom God chooses not to regenerate* is not any different in its eternal effects from eternal punishment apart from an offer of salvation.

The issue here is the justice of God. Is God unjust in His treatment of Satan and his angelic followers? If not, then how can anyone legitimately conclude that God is unjust in damning *any* ethical rebel whom He has chosen not to regenerate? The issue here is *the justice of condemning any rebel **inescapably** to eternal punishment without a prior possibility of his repenting*. If such inescapable condemnation is fully justified in Satan's case, why not in the case of human rebels?

And if it is unjust in the case of Satan's human followers, don't we have to argue that it is also unjust of God in Satan's case? Satan would *love* that argument!

For further study: Acts 5:31; 11:18; II Tim. 2:25-26.

Question 17
Aren't Men Ordained in Advance to Eternal Life?

> **For so hath the Lord commanded us, saying, I have set thee to be a light of the Gentiles, that thou shouldest be for salvation unto the ends of the earth. And when the Gentiles heard this, they were glad, and glorified the word of the Lord: and as many as were ordained to eternal life believed** (Acts 13:47, 48).

The text is clear. There were Gentiles who heard the preaching of Paul and Barnabas. Some were ordained to eternal life, and some were not. "**As many as were ordained to eternal life believed.**" It could not be any clearer. Not one fewer believed the gospel of salvation than had been ordained to eternal life, and not one more. *Just as many as:* a "one-to-one" relationship.

Is there a random aspect to salvation? Are some men chosen by God to attain the status of adopted sons, and then they thwart God's choice, either by refusing to believe the gospel initially, or by believing, becoming converts, and then departing from the faith? Are others not ordained to eternal life, but somehow, by the grace of God (yet not by His plan), believe the message and receive salvation? In other words, is there biblical evidence to indicate that the relationship between those ordained for salvation and those who attain it is not one to one? Is what is described in Acts 13:48 itself random—a unique event which is not representative of God's plan of salvation? In short, is there a discrepancy between those ordained and those who are actually converted?

Questionable Answer

"The Greek word translated as 'ordained' is mistranslated. It really means something like 'predisposed to.' There is only an inclination to be saved. There is no one-to-one relationship between God's ordaining a person to be saved—which God does not do, in any case—and a person's response."

My Reply: Try to locate any translation of the Bible which does not use "ordained" or some variation of "ordained." The American Standard Version says "ordained." The Revised Standard Version says "ordained." The New English Bible says "marked out." The New American Standard says "appointed." The New International Version says "appointed." The verb is passive.

Is there any reason to believe that what is described in the Book of Acts, the story of the spread of the gospel in the earliest days, should not be understood as representative of the effects of the gospel in general? Is there some reason to believe that the testimony of Luke in Acts concerning the early church's experience is in no way comparable to the church's experience throughout history? Is there some biblical reason why Luke would insert into his account of the conversion of the Gentiles of Antioch information about God's ordination of those to be saved, if such information is historically unique—a one-time event which cannot be understood as universal? If we argue that Luke's account doesn't describe a universal phenomenon, aren't we saying that God has altered the way of salvation? Dare we say this?

For further study: Rom. 11:2, 5-7; I Cor. 1:27-31; II Tim. 2:10.

Question 18
Doesn't God Compel Men to Believe in Jesus?

No man can come to me, except the Father which hath sent me draw [drag] him: and I will raise him up at the last day (John 6:44).

The context makes it clear that Jesus was speaking here of eternal life. He was not speaking of a general call to all men to listen to the gospel. He was speaking about God's drawing men so close to Jesus ethically that they will be raised up at the last day. In other words, He was speaking of salvation.

The Greek word which is translated here as "draw" could be translated as "**drag.**" (It could also be translated as "**attract.**") But the point is the same, whichever of the three English words is used to express the meaning of the Greek: God the Father brings a person to faith in Christ.

Didn't Jesus say that "**I am the way, the truth, and the life: no man cometh unto the Father, but by me**" (John 14:6)? Yes, He did. So if we are to take His words seriously, we must affirm a *reciprocal relationship:* God the Father alone can draw men to a saving faith in His Son, yet apart from the Son, no man comes ethically to God the Father.

Can anyone come to faith in God without the initial act of compulsion—dragging—by the Father? If God the Father refuses to draw the person to Christ, can anyone attain salvation? No, says the Bible: ". . . **no man can come unto me, except it were given unto him of my Father**" (John 6:65).

Questionable Answer

"God the Father is involved in salvation. But He is only partially active. He leads the unbeliever to Christ, but He does not *drag* him to Christ. That word is too strong. It is more of a mild attraction. He just *introduces* men to His Son. From then on, it is up to them to decide."

My Reply: Why did Jesus use a word that points to dragging? If this were the only verse in the Bible that pointed to active predestination by God in saving men, then the use of a softer, less active word to translate the term might be acceptable. But this is another example of God's *active* role in salvation on the one hand, and the *exclusionary* aspect on the other. If He ignores an unsaved man—if He refuses to draw him to His Son—then there is no hope for that man. After Adam's rebellion, *the exclusion is automatic!*

Jesus said: "**Ye have not chosen me, but I have chosen you**" (John 15:16a). This act of free choice is not man's act, but God's. Can we legitimately speak of man's free will and God's free will at the same time? How? If Jesus says that He chooses us, and men do not choose Him, then *the free agent is God*, who elects men and chooses them, not man. When God the Father chooses those who will serve His Son, how can they refuse this obligation? If God the Father has ordained them to serve His son, then how can the person refuse to serve? Men are *dragged* into loving service.

For further study: Deut. 30:6; Ezek. 36:26-27; John 1:13; 3:3-8; 5:21; Eph. 2:1, 5; Col. 2:13.

Question 19
Didn't God Choose Us Long before We Accepted Him?

> But we are bound to give thanks alway to God for you, brethren beloved of the Lord, because God hath from the beginning chosen you to salvation through sanctification of the Spirit and belief of the truth: Whereunto he called you by our gospel, to the obtaining of the glory of our Lord Jesus Christ (II Thessalonians 2:13-14).

First, God chooses a person as His own. He does this **"from the beginning,"** meaning at least from the beginning of time, before the foundation of the world. The person was not consulted about this decision by God. It is a wholly active decision by God, since God alone existed at the beginning. Where was man's response in the days before the creation of man?

Second, God calls men to believe in His Son, Jesus Christ. He calls men by means of the gospel message. This takes place in time and on earth. It is God's historical and personal confirmation of the choice He made from the beginning. *God, not man, is the free active agent in regeneration.* Jesus said:

> **Ye have not chosen me, but I have chosen you, and ordained you, that ye should go and bring forth fruit, and that your fruit should remain: that whatsoever ye shall ask of the Father in my name, he may give it you** (John 15:16).

Questionable Answer

"Paul was writing to the church of Thessalonica, not to specific individuals. His letter was also aimed at the church as a whole through history, but not to specific individuals. God chose the church as a plural whole for salvation. This does not mean that any specific person was actually chosen by God from the beginning."

My Reply: If God chose the church as a whole, why was He confident that there would ever be a church? If He did not select specific individuals to fill this invisible church, then he selected a box—a potentially *empty* box. In fact, it was a *predictably* empty box, for He would have had to rely on the hearts of unregenerate, rebellious men to choose Him, in order to fill up the church as a whole. But unregenerate men don't receive spiritual ideas (Question 20).

Do unregenerate men choose Christ? Christ said specifically that He chose His followers; they did not choose Him. Did He also choose "followers in general" but not specific followers? Did His "followers in general" choose Him? How do "followers in general" do anything? *Specific people make decisions, not organizations in general.* People choose or fail to choose, and are rewarded or cursed by God in terms of their choices; "institutions in general," apart from specific members, don't exist. In any case, nobody chose Him; He chose people—the people He loved. The text is clear: the brethren who were *"loved of the Lord"* were chosen by God *"from the beginning."*

For further study: Rom. 9:6-26; 1 Pet. 1:1-2; 2:9-10.

Question 20
How Can an Unregenerate Man Accept Christ?

> **But the natural man receiveth not the things of the Spirit of God: for they are foolishness unto him: neither can he know them, because they are spiritually discerned** (I Corinthians 2:14).

The text is clear. The "natural man," meaning the unregenerate person, doesn't receive the things of the spirit. All such topics are regarded by him as foolishness. "**But we preach Christ crucified, unto the Jews a stumblingblock, and unto the Greeks foolishness; but unto them which are called, both Jews and Greeks, Christ the power of God, and the wisdom of God** (I Corinthians 1:23-24). The unregenerate person refuses to believe in such "foolishness."

The contrast is between the *natural* man and the *called* man, meaning the regenerate man. Why does one man regard the gospel as foolishness, and the other man recognize the power of Jesus Christ? The message is the same. There is only one explanation: each man interprets the message differently. What determines each interpretation? Isn't it the *presuppositions* each man has concerning the true nature of the universe: God, man, and law? The natural man *assumes* the gospel is foolish.

If the natural man interprets the gospel as foolishness, how can he ever be converted to faith in Christ? By grace (Ephesians 2:8). He is first regenerated by God; *then* He accepts the gospel. God must regenerate him—an act of sovereign grace—if he is to become an "unnatural" man capable of saving faith.

Questionable Answer

"The Bible says, 'Whosoever will, may come.' Anyone may come to Christ who wills to. Whether he exercises saving faith or not is a matter of free will on his part, not God's electing grace. The natural man sees the truth well enough to make an autonomous decision."

My Reply: Just for the record, the Bible *doesn't* say "Whosoever will, may come," although Revelation 22:17 says something close. The question still must be answered: Can an unregenerate person *will* to come to Christ? Is his will "free," meaning *autonomous*?

What does I Corinthians 2:14 say? Does Paul give any warrant for believing that the unregenerate man is capable of properly interpreting the gospel message, and then responding in faith to its offer of salvation? Can the unregenerate Jew do it? Can the unregenerate Greek? The text says *no*.

Both the "called Jew" and the "called Greek" *can* interpret the message properly. What is the difference in response, "natural" vs. "called"? *God's electing grace.* God has elected some before the foundation of the world (Ephesians 1:4). He has not elected others. **"Therefore hath he mercy on whom he will have mercy, and whom he will he hardeneth"** (Romans 9:18). It's God's decision, not man's, since the natural man cannot receive the things of the spirit. We are first saved by God's sovereign grace, and immediately we accept Christ. Redeemed men *believe through grace* (Acts 18:27b). Without electing grace, men cannot believe.

For further study: John 6:44, 65; 8:34; 10:26; Rom. 3:10-12; 6:20; 8:7-8; Eph. 4:17-19; II Tim. 2:25-26; Titus 3:3.

Question 21
Could the Authorities Have Acted Righteously and Released Jesus?

For of a truth against thy holy child Jesus, whom thou hast anointed, both Herod, and Pontius Pilate, with the Gentiles, and the people of Israel, were gathered together, for to do whatsoever thy hand and thy counsel determined before to be done (Acts 4:27-28).

This prayer of the early apostles before the chief priests and elders was made publicly to God. They affirmed by this prayer the sovereignty of the God of the Bible over the affairs of that day. It was a reminder to the rulers that they were under God's authority, and they could do nothing to thwart His designs, even when they thought that they were overcoming His designs and His people.

The rulers released Barabas, not Christ. The crowd yelled "Give us Barabas," and Pilate did. Did they overturn God's plan for the ages? Hardly; they made a decision to crucify Christ, the *turning point* of the ages. This turning point had been foreordained before the foundation of the world.

Something similar happened to Joseph when his brothers sold him into slavery. He saved their lives from famine years later. He said to them: "**As for you, ye thought evil against me; but God meant it unto good**" (Genesis 50:20). God ordains the good; men plan evil; but the historical event is the same. The greatest good and the greatest evil—the cross—was ordained.

Questionable Answer

"God did not really foreordain the personal decisions of men that led directly but not inescapably to the crucifixion. The crucifixion as an event was inevitable, but not the events that led to it. The specific decisions made by the authorities were made in perfect free will; God did not ordain them. Only the *general event* was foreordained, *not* the *specific decisions* of men that led directly to the general event."

My Reply: If the events leading to a particular event are not foreordained, but the event itself is—to the very day—then how was God sure that the foreordained event would, in fact, result from the decisions of the leaders? If they could have released Jesus, how was the crucifixion inevitable?

The text, however, is more specific: Herod, Pontius Pilate, Gentiles, and Israelites were all gathered together, **"For to do whatsoever thy hand and thy counsel determined before to be done."** It was not simply the crucifixion which was foreordained; it was the *decisions of the people* who were gathered in Jerusalem that week. **"Him, being delivered by the determinate counsel and foreknowledge of God, ye have taken, and by wicked hands have crucified and slain"** (Acts 2:23). The events that led directly to the crucifixion were as foreordained as the crucifixion. How can an event be determined and not the acts leading to it? Was God going to rely on the autonomous will of men as the basis of the most important event in history?

For further study: John 7:30; 8:20; 19:11; Rev. 13:8; 17:8.

Question 22
Isn't God's Grace Irresistible?

> **[It is God] who hath saved us, and called us with an holy calling, not according to our works, but according to his own purpose and grace, which was given us in Christ Jesus before the world began** (II Timothy 1:9).

God's purpose was to create a people called by His name. These people have a *holy calling*, meaning a God-assigned task to subdue the earth—*to exercise dominion* in His name under His authority, both before the final judgment and after (Genesis 1:27-28).

This assignment was in the plan of God before He created the world. The rebellion of man was also known to God and part of that plan. Therefore, Paul tells us, God granted His people grace in Jesus Christ before the creation. Paul's words are quite plain.

If God granted His people grace before time began, how can any grace-designated man escape that grace? Aren't we talking about *irresistible grace?* Can man thwart the purpose of God? Can any man reject this specific calling to salvation, through the use of something called "free will"? If so, then what becomes of God's purpose to select people to serve Him in a holy calling?

Is the *exercise of faith* a *work of man*? It *can't* be a work. Doesn't Paul say specifically that God selects His people, not on the basis of their works, but by His grace? Isn't saving faith an *irresistible gift*?

Questionable Answer

"God predestines the church as a whole to believe in Christ and to carry out its holy calling. But God never predestined individual members. At the most, He predestined a specific number of believers over time, but He selected them in terms of His original knowledge of whether they would exercise faith in Christ. Men can reject the offer of salvation. God does not force them to believe."

My Reply: The purpose of God is to separate out from fallen humanity a remnant, His people. They are to have a holy calling specified by God. But to achieve His purposes, God must specify each individual's calling. He has planned to achieve certain goals, many of which were announced by God to His people in the form of *prophecies*. Won't God see to it that His prophecies come to pass? Doesn't God *make* His prophecies come to pass?

The Bible doesn't say that God predestined a *group in general* apart from predestinating *members in particular*. The Bible speaks only of God's granting His grace to us in Christ, irrespective of any works we perform. How can we talk about a *work of faith* or a *work of unbelief* as the foundation of salvation or damnation? Isn't the issue *God's sovereign grace?* We are saved by grace through faith (a gift of God), not by works.

If man is saved by his own autonomous work of faith, then the *lie* of Satan is true: *man is partially autonomous;* he has become a little god.

For further study: I Ki. 8:58; Jer. 31:3; John 8:36, 42; Eph. 2:1-10; II Cor. 4:6; Titus 3:5-6.

Question 23
Isn't the Will of God Absolutely Sovereign?

He doeth according to His will in the army of heaven, and among the inhabitants of the earth: and none can stay his hand, or say unto him, What doest thou? (Daniel 4:35).

The sovereignty of God is asserted throughout the Bible. The question is: Does God voluntarily withdraw Himself from millions of events, especially the event of salvation, but also all evil acts of men, and thereby turn control over these historical events to men or angels? Does He abdicate from His position of total potential power, in order to open zones of pure freedom for men? Does He bring His will to pass only by intervening into history sporadically?

In Hebrews 1:3, we read of Christ that He *upholds* all things by the word of his power. All things? He is **"above all, and through all, and in you all"** (Ephesians 4:6). God spoke through Isaiah: **"Remember the former things of old: for I am God, and there is none else; I am God, and there is none like me, Declaring the end from the beginning, and from ancient times the things that are not yet done, saying, My counsel shall stand, and I will do all my pleasure"** (46:9-10).

How powerful is God's word? **"So shall my word be that goeth forth out of my mouth: it shall not return unto me void, but it shall accomplish that which I please, and it shall prosper in the thing whereto I sent it"** (Isaiah 55:11). Comprehensive!

Questionable Answer

"God prophesies concerning the future, and the events do take place. But *in between* the prophesied events, God leaves men free to make their own decisions. These decisions do not lead inevitably to the prophesied event, or else they would themselves be inevitable. Instead, God intervenes occasionally to bring men's events into line with His specific purposes."

My Reply: Can't events be two-fold: 1) God's purpose and 2) man's purpose? Can't the same event be the product of God's sovereign plan, yet involve man's responsible decision? Can't men plan evil and God bring good from it? Can't an event be predestined by God and still be a matter of human responsibility? If not, then why was Christ's crucifixion a blessing from God, and at the same time, an act of evil on the part of rebellious men?

If God's providence undergirds all creation, shouldn't Christians be confident that all things work for the good of those who are called according to His purpose? Shouldn't they rest confidently in the absolute sovereignty of God? Why argue that most events are determined solely by men, and not by God? Look at Egypt: **"For it was of the Lord to harden their hearts, that they should come against Israel in battle, that he might destroy them utterly, and that they might have no favor, but that he might destroy them, as the Lord commanded Moses"** (Joshua 11:20).

For further study: Gen. 41:32; I Kings 22:28, 34; Ps. 24:1; 47:7-8; 103:19; Prov. 16:33; 21:1; Isa. 45:7; 46:10-11; Lam. 3:37-38.

Question 24
Isn't Faith in Christ the Gift of God?

And the servant of the Lord must not strive; but be gentle unto all men, apt to teach, patient, In meekness instructing those that oppose themselves; if God peradventure will give them repentance to the acknowledging of the truth; and that they may recover themselves out of the snare of the devil, who are taken captive by him at his will (II Timothy 2:24-26).

God *gives* men repentance. Paul couldn't be clearer. The faith through which the grace of God comes is itself an aspect of the grace of God. It isn't an *autonomous work* which *unregenerate* man brings before God in order to receive salvation. It *is* a gift from God. James wrote: **"Every good gift and every perfect gift is from above, and cometh down from the Father of lights, with whom is no variableness, neither shadow of turning"** (James 1:17). Salvation is no exception. It is all God's grace.

This is why we can legitimately pray for the conversion of others. God is in a position to grant us that prayer request. Yes, we should add, "If it be thy will, O Lord." But bear in mind that it's *His* will which is decisive, not the will of the person we are praying for.

"His divine power hath given unto us all things that pertain unto life and godliness, through the knowledge of him that hath called us to glory and virtue" (II Peter 1:3). *All* things that pertain to life and godliness? Even salvation? Yes!

Questionable Answer

"If exercising faith is simply an automatic response to God's offer of salvation, then 'salvation by faith alone' is meaningless. Salvation would then be 'by grace through grace,' rather than 'by grace through faith.' Faith is different from grace; man is responsible to respond to God's offer of salvation. He must choose for himself."

My Reply: Is faith a work or a gift? If it is a work—something of man's own doing which man brings to God in order to attain salvation—then are we justified by works? If it is a gift, then the phrase "by grace through faith" means that *God initiates the offer, but then He enables man to respond*. The natural man must first become the spiritual man, so that he can understand and respond in faith to the message—a message which is foolishness to the unregenerate (I Corinthians 2:14-15). *Then* he responds in faith. The words "through faith" simply point to man's response—*a God-ordained, inescapable response*—to God's offer.

If this interpretation is incorrect, then what are we to make of Paul's words to Timothy? He also wrote to Titus: "**Not by works of righteousness which we have done, but according to his mercy he saved us, by the washing of regeneration, and renewing of the Holy Ghost**" (Titus 3:5). Is it right to look at faith as if it were a "work of righteousness"? Do we work our way into heaven? Shouldn't we take the words of the Bible seriously and affirm that faith itself is God's gift, as surely as grace is?

For further study: Matt. 16:16-17; John 6:44-45; Acts 5:31; 11:18; 18:27; Eph. 2:8-9; Phil. 1:29; Heb. 12:2; II Pet. 1:1.

Question 25
Did Christ Die for All Men?

For God so loved the world, that he gave his only begotten Son, that whosoever believeth in him should not perish, but have everlasting life (John 3:16).

We have already asked the question about "whosoever will," which is a variant of "whosoever believeth" (Question 20). The question raises the issue of the ability of unregenerate men to come to saving faith in Christ, if the natural man receives not the things of the Spirit (I Corinthians 2:14).

To understand John 3:16, you need to have come to grips with the previous questions in this book. What is "the world" that God loves? Is it "all men in general"? Then why did He despise Esau and promise to curse him, before Esau had done good or evil? Why do Christ's prayers of intercession convert some but not all? If He prays for all men to be saved, and some resist and perish, can we say that Christ's prayers are efficacious? Do they really work? Or are the results random?

God loves the whole creation. He sustains it moment by moment. This is the doctrine of *providence*. He sustained it after Adam rebelled. Why? He promised to bring death to Adam, yet He allowed the world to continue. He preserved it for the sake of the as-yet unborn elect. He preserved it for the sake of Jesus Christ, His incarnate Son, who came to die for His chosen elect. God loves His creation; He does not love all men, irrespective of their relation to Jesus Christ.

Questionable Answer

"Jesus died for all mankind. Some accept, and others refuse, but He died so that all men might experience the possibility of being saved from hell. This is the meaning of 'the world.' It means 'all men.' God brings the world under judgment. It is not saved; men are saved."

My Reply: All good things that we receive are gifts from God (James 1:17). Is life such a gift? Then it is a gift from God. Do unrighteous men deserve gifts? No, they deserve death. Do they receive good gifts? Yes, they do. God gives them gifts for the sake of the elect, so that life can prosper through the co-operation of both elect and unregenerate. He also gives them gifts *in order to heap extra coals of fire on their heads* when they do not respond in faith—the reason Paul gave us for treating sinners decently (Romans 12:20). Look it up!

God sends rain on sinners and saints alike (Matthew 5:45). This can be called God's *common grace*. It is common to all men. But this says nothing about God's *special grace* to individual sinners whom God has chosen to regenerate, by grace. The fact that God gives unmerited, *non-saving* gifts to all men in no way proves that anyone can respond to the equally unmerited offer of salvation. Both kinds of grace—common and saving—are possible only because of Christ's work. So all men benefit *generally* from Christ's death, but only Christ's elect benefit eternally (see Question 75).

For further study: Matt. 20:28; John 6:37-39; 10:11, 15, 26; Acts 20:28; Eph. 1:4-7; 5:25-27; Heb. 5:9.

Supplement to Part I:
Historic Creeds

Your instructors may take the following approach when you begin to ask them these questions, or when you show this book to them. They may say: "This material is heretical. Only a handful of people in the history of the church have ever believed such things about the sovereignty of God. What I have taught you is what most Christians have always believed for almost 2,000 years."

This answer is incorrect. On the contrary, what the great theological leaders of the church have proclaimed is that God, and God alone, is sovereign over His creation, and therefore God predestinates men to heaven or hell. Man is morally powerless to accept God's salvation unless God specifically empowers him to believe in Christ. This was certainly the teaching of St. Augustine, and he wrote a lengthy criticism of a man who taught the opposite, the heretic Pelagius. You can read his analysis in Volume V of *The Nicene and Post-Nicene Fathers*, edited by Philip Schaff (Grand Rapids, Michigan: Eerdmans Publishing Co.): *Saint Augustine's Anti-Pelagian Works*. This was also the teaching of Martin Luther. You can read his devastating criticism of the humanist Erasmus, who argued as Pelagius did, that man has free will to accept or reject the gospel. Luther's response is titled *The Bondage of the Will* (1525). It is one of the most important documents of the Protestant Reformation. It is still in print.

This was certainly the belief of Charles H. Spurgeon,

the great Baptist preacher of the late nineteenth century. He preached a famous sermon on "Election," based on II Thessalonians 2:13-14, which is reprinted in his *New Park Street Pulpit*, Vol. I. His position is summarized in the book by Iain Murray, *The Forgotten Spurgeon* (Carlisle, Pennsylvania: Banner of Truth Trust). But be sure to get the original versions or photographic reprints of the originals. In the 1950's, "expurgated" editions of Spurgeon's writings were reprinted by an unscrupulous fundamentalist leader who deliberately removed all references to predestination from the revised sermons by Spurgeon (and admitted that he did it in a letter I have personally seen). As I've said, there has been a deliberate effort on the part of many instructors to mislead students with respect to certain doctrines of the faith.

I have selected relevant statements from a number of ecclesiastical traditions to prove my case: Episcopalian (Anglican), Baptist, Congregationalist, Lutheran, Reformed, and Presbyterian. Anyone who tells you that the sovereignty of God hasn't been the primary belief of *orthodox* Christians through the ages is either lying, or he is ignorant about what he is saying, or he defines "orthodox" differently from what the historic creeds have taught. But in any case, the history of the church stands against him. Will it stand against you, too?

Baptist

Chapter III—*Of God's Decrees*

1. God hath (Isa. 56:10; Eph. 1:11; Heb. 6:17; Rom. 9:15, 18) decreed in himself, from all eternity, by the most wise and holy counsel of his own will, freely and unchangeably, all things whatsoever come to pass; yet so as thereby is God neither the author of sin (James 1:13; I John 1:5) nor hath fellowship with any therein; nor is violence offered to the will

of the creature, nor yet is the liberty or contingency of second causes taken away, but rather (Acts 4:27, 28; John 19:11) established; in which appears his wisdom in disposing all things, and power and faithfulness (Num. 23:19; Eph. 1:3, 4, 5) in accomplishing his decree.

2. Although God knoweth whatsoever may or can come to pass upon all (Acts 15:18) supposed conditions; yet hath he not decreed anything, because he (Rom. 9:11, 13, 16, 18) foresaw it as future, or as that which would come to pass upon such conditions.

3. By the decree of God, for the manifestation of his glory, (I Tim. 5:21; Matt. 25:41) some men and angels are predestinated or foreordained to eternal life, through Jesus Christ, to the (Eph. 1:5, 6) praise of his glorious grace; others being left to act in their sin to their (Rom. 9:22, 23; Jude 4) just condemnation, to the praise of his glorious justice.

4. These angels and men thus predestinated and foreordained, are particularly and unchangeably designed; and their (II Tim. 2:19; John 23:18) number so certain, and definite, that it cannot be either increased or diminished.

5. Those of mankind (Eph. 1:4, 9, 11; Rom. 8:30; II Tim. 1:9; I Thess. 5:9) that are predestinated to life, God, before the foundation of the world was laid, according to his eternal and immutable purpose and the secret counsel and good pleasure of his will, hath chosen in Christ unto everlasting glory, out of his mere free grace and love (Rom. 19:13, 16; Eph. 2:5, 12); without any other things in the creature as a condition or cause moving him thereunto.

6. As God hath appointed the elect unto glory, so he hath, by the eternal and most free purpose of his will, foreordained (I Pet. 1:2; II Thess. 2:13) all the means thereunto, wherefore they who are elected, being fallen in Adam (I Thess. 5:9, 10), are redeemed by Christ, are effectually (Rom. 8:30; II Thess. 2:13) called unto faith in Christ, by his Spirit working in due season, are justified, adopted, sanctified, and kept by his power through faith (I Pet. 1:5) unto salvation; neither are any other redeemed by Christ, or effectually called, justified, adopted, sanctified, and saved, but the elect (John 10:26;

17:9; 6:64) only.

7. The doctrine of this high mystery of predestination is to be handled with special prudence and care, that men attending the will of God revealed in his word and yielding obedience thereunto, may, from the certainty of their effectual vocation, be assured of their (I Thess. 1:4, 5; II Pet. 1:10) eternal election; so shall this doctrine afford matter (Eph. 1:6; Rom. 11:33) of praise, reverence, and admiration of God, and (Rom. 11:5, 6, 20) of humility, diligence, and abundant (Luke 10:20) consolation to all that sincerely obey the gospel.

Chapter IX—*Of Free Will*

1. God hath indued the will of man with that natural liberty and power of acting upon choice, that it is (Matt. 17:12; James 1:14; Deut. 30:19) neither forced, nor by any necessity of nature determined to do good or evil.

2. Man, in his state of innocency, had freedom and power to will and to do that (Eccl. 7:29) which was good, and well pleasing to God; but yet (Gen. 3:6) was mutable, so that he might fall from it.

3. Man, by his fall into a state of sin, hath wholly lost (Rom. 5:6; 8:7) all ability of will to any spiritual good accompanying salvation; so as a natural man, being altogether averse from that good, and (Eph. 2:1, 5) dead in sin, is not able, by his own strength, to (Tit. 3:3, 4, 5; John 6:44) convert himself or to prepare himself thereunto.

4. When God converts a sinner, and translates him into the state of grace (Col. 1:13; John 8:36), he freeth him from his natural bondage under sin, and by his grace alone enables him (Phil. 2:13) freely to will and to do that which is spiritually good; yet so as that, by reason of his (Rom. 7:15, 18, 19, 21, 23) remaining corruptions, he doth not perfectly nor only will that which is good, but doth also will that which is evil.

5. The will of man is made (Eph. 4:13) perfectly and immutably free to God alone in the state of glory only.

Chapter X—*Of Effectual Calling*

1. Those whom God hath predestinated unto life he is pleased, in his appointed and accepted time, effectually to call (Rom. 8:30; 11:7; Eph. 1:10, 11; II Thess. 2:13, 14) by his word and Spirit, out of that state of sin and death in which they are by nature, to grace and salvation (Eph. 1:1-6) by Jesus Christ; enlightening their minds, spiritually and savingly, to (Acts 26:18; Eph. 1:17, 18) understand the things of God; taking away their (Ezek. 36:26) heart of stone, and giving unto them a heart of flesh; renewing their wills, and by his almighty power determining them (Deut. 30:6; Ezek. 36:27; Eph. 1:19) to that which is good, and effectually drawing them to Jesus Christ; yet so as they come (Ps. 110:3; Cant. 1:4) most freely, being made willing by his grace.

2. This effectual call is of God's free and special grace alone (II Tim. 1:9; Eph. 2:8), not from anything at all foreseen in man, nor from any power or agency in the creature, coworking with his special grace (I Cor. 2:14; Eph. 2:5; John 5:25), the creature being wholly passive therein, being quickened and renewed by the Holy Spirit, he is thereby enabled to answer this call, and to embrace the grace offered and conveyed in it, and that by no less (Eph. 1:19, 20) power than that which raised up Christ from the dead.

3. Elect infants dying in infancy, are (John 3:3, 5, 6) regenerated and saved by Christ through the Spirit; who worketh when, and where, and (John 3:8) how he pleaseth; so also are all other elect persons, who are incapable of being outwardly called by the ministry of the word.

4. Others not elected, although they may be called by the ministry of the word (Matt. 13:20, 21; 22:14; Heb. 6:4, 5) and may have some common operations of the Spirit, yet not being effectually drawn by the Father, they neither will nor can truly (John 6:44, 45, 65; I John 2:24, 25) come to Christ, and therefore cannot be saved: much less can men that receive not the Christian religion (Acts 4:12; John 4:22; John 17:3) be saved; be they never so diligent to frame their lives according to the light of nature and the law of that religion they do profess.

London Confession, 1689

It is no novelty, then, that I am preaching; no new doctrine. I love to proclaim these strong old doctrines, which are called by nickname Calvinism, but which are surely and verily the revealed truth of God as it is in Christ Jesus. By this truth I make a pilgrimage into the past, and as I go, I see father after father, confessor after confessor, martyr after martyr, standing up to shake hands with me. Were I a Pelagian, or a believer in the doctrine of free-will, I should have to walk for centuries all alone. Here and there a heretic of no very honourable character might rise up and call me brother. But taking these things to be the standard of my faith, I see the land of the ancients peopled with my brethren—I behold multitudes who confess the same as I do, and acknowledge that this is the religion of God's own church.

Charles Spurgeon
The New Park Street Pulpit, Vol. I (1856)

There is no such thing as preaching Christ and Him crucified, unless we preach what nowadays is called Calvinism. It is a nickname to call it Calvinism; Calvinism is the gospel, and nothing else. I do not believe we can preach the gospel, if we do not preach justification by faith without works: not unless we preach the sovereignty of God in His dispensation of grace; nor unless we exalt the electing, unchangeable, eternal, immutable, conquering love of Jehovah; nor do I think we can preach the gospel unless we base it upon the special and particular redemption of His elect and chosen people which Christ wrought out upon the cross; nor can I comprehend a gospel which lets saints fall away after they are called, and suffers the children of God to be burned in the fires of damnation after having once believed in Jesus. Such a gospel I abhor.

Charles Spurgeon
Autobiography (1897)

Congregationalist

Chapter 3—*Of God's Eternal Decree*

1. God from all eternity did by the most wise and holy counsel of his own will, freely and unchangeably ordain whatsoever comes to pass: yet so, as thereby neither is God the author of sin, nor is violence offered to the will of the creatures, nor is the liberty or contingency of second causes taken away, but rather established.

2. Although God knows whatsoever may or can come to pass upon all supposed conditions, yet hath he not decreed any thing, because he foresaw it as future, or as that which would come to pass upon such conditions.

3. By the decree of God for the manifestation of his glory, some men and angels are predestinated unto everlasting life, and others fore-ordained to everlasting death.

4. These angels and men thus predestinated, and fore-ordained, are particularly and unchangeably designed, and their number is so certain and definite, that it cannot be either increased or diminished.

5. Those of mankind that are predestinated unto life, God, before the foundation of the world was laid, according to his eternal and immutable purpose, and the secret counsel and good pleasure of his will, hath chosen in Christ unto everlasting glory, out of his mere free grace and love, without any foresight of faith or good works, or perseverance in either of them, or any other thing in the creature, as conditions or causes moving him thereunto, and all to the praise of his glorious grace.

6. As God hath appointed the elect unto glory, so hath he by the eternal and most free purpose of his will fore-ordained all the means thereunto. Wherefore they who are elected, being fallen in Adam, are redeemed by Christ, are effectually called unto faith in Christ by the Spirit working in due season, are justified, adopted, sanctified, and kept by his power, through faith, unto salvation. Neither are any other redeemed by Christ, or effectually called, justified,

adopted, sanctified and saved, but the elect only.

7. The rest of mankind God was pleased, according to the unsearchable counsel of his own will, whereby he extendeth or withholdeth mercy, as he pleaseth, for the glory of his sovereign power over his creatures, to pass by and to ordain them to dishonour and wrath for their sin, to the praise of his glorious justice.

8. The doctrine of this high mystery of predestination is to be handled with special prudence and care, that men attending the will of God revealed in his Word, and yielding obedience thereunto, may from the certainty of their effectual vocation, be assured of their eternal election. So shall this doctrine afford matter of praise, reverence and admiration of God, and of humility, diligence, and abundant consolation to all that sincerely obey the Gospel.

Chapter 9—*Of Free Will*

1. God hath endued the will of man with that natural liberty and power of acting upon choice that it is neither forced, nor by any absolute necessity of nature determined to do good or evil.

2. Man in his state of innocency had freedom and power to will and to do that which was good and well-pleasing to God; but yet mutably, so that he might fall from it.

3. Man by his fall into a state of sin, hath wholly lost all ability of will to any spiritual good accompanying salvation; so as a natural man being altogether averse from that good, and dead in sin, is not able by his own strength to convert himself, or to prepare himself thereunto.

4. When God converts a sinner, and translates him into the state of grace, he freeth him from his natural bondage under sin, and by his grace alone enables him freely to will and to do that which is spiritually good; yet so as that, by reason of his remaining corruption, he doth not perfectly nor only will that which is good, but doth also will that which is evil.

5. The will of man is made perfectly and immutably free to do good alone in the state of glory only.

Chapter 10—*Of Effectual Calling*

1. All those whom God hath predestinated unto life, and those only, he is pleased in his appointed and accepted time effectually to call by his Word and Spirit, out of that state of sin and death in which they are by nature, to grace and salvation by Jesus Christ; enlightening their minds spiritually and savingly to understand the things of God, taking away their heart of stone, and giving unto them an heart of flesh; renewing their wills, and by his almighty power determining them to that which is good; and effectually drawing them to Jesus Christ; yet so, as they come most freely, being made willing by his grace.

2. This effectual call is of God's free and special grace alone, not from any thing at all foreseen in man, who is altogether passive therein, until being quickened and renewed by the Holy Spirit he is thereby enabled to answer this call, and to embrace the grace offered and conveyed in it.

3. Elect infants dying in infancy, are regenerated and saved by Christ, who worketh when, and where, and how he pleaseth: so also are all other elect persons who are incapable of being outwardly called by the ministry of the Word.

4. Others not elected, although they may be called by the ministry of the Word, and may have some common operations of the Spirit, yet not being effectually drawn by the Father, they neither do nor can come unto Christ, and therefore cannot be saved: much less can men not professing the Christian religion, be saved in any other way whatsoever, be they never so diligent to frame their lives according to the light of nature, and the law of that religion they do profess: and to assert and maintain that they may, is very pernicious, and to be detested.

The Savoy Confession of Faith, 1658

Episcopalian (Anglican)

X. *Of Free Will*

The condition of Man after the fall of Adam is such, that he cannot turn and prepare himself, by his own natural strength and good works, to faith, and calling upon God. Wherefore we have no power to do good works pleasant and acceptable to God, without the grace of God by Christ preventing us, that we may have a good will, and working with us, when we have that good will.

XVII. *Of Predestination and Election*

Predestination to Life is the everlasting purpose of God, whereby (before the foundations of the world were laid) he hath constantly decreed by his counsel secret to us, to deliver from curse and damnation those whom he hath chosen in Christ out of mankind, and to bring them by Christ to everlasting salvation, as vessels made to honour. Wherefore, they which be endued with so excellent a benefit of God, be called according to God's purpose by his Spirit working in due season: they through Grace obey the calling: they be justified freely: they be made sons of God by adoption: they be made like the image of his only-begotten Son Jesus Christ: they walk religiously in good works, and at length, by God's mercy, they attain to everlasting felicity . . . the godly consideration of Predestination, and our Election in Christ, is full of sweet, pleasant, and unspeakable comfort to godly persons, and such as feel in themselves the working of the Spirit of Christ, mortifying the works of the flesh, and their earthly members, and drawing up their mind to high and heavenly things, as well because it doth greatly establish and confirm their faith of eternal Salvation to be enjoyed through Christ as because it doth fervently kindle their love towards God.

The Thirty-Nine Articles, 1563

Lutheran

It is, then, fundamentally necessary and wholesome for Christians to know that God foreknows nothing contingently, but that He foresees, purposes, and does all things according to His own immutable, eternal and infallible will.

The Christian's chief and only comfort in every adversity lies in knowing that God does not lie, but brings all things to pass immutably, and that His will cannot be resisted, altered or impeded.

God has surely promised His grace to the humbled: that is, to those who mourn over and despair of themselves. But a man cannot be thoroughly humbled till he realizes that his salvation is utterly beyond his own powers, counsels, efforts, will and works, and depends absolutely on the will, counsel, pleasure and work of Another—God alone. As long as he is persuaded that he can make even the smallest contribution to his salvation, he remains self-confident and does not utterly despair of himself, and so is not humbled before God; but plans out for himself (or at least hopes and longs for) a position, an occasion, a work, which shall bring him final salvation. But he who is out of doubt that his destiny depends entirely on the will of God despairs entirely of himself, chooses nothing for himself, but waits for God to work in him; and such a man is very near to grace for his salvation.

Martin Luther, 1525

Presbyterian

Chapter III—*Of God's Eternal Decree*

I. God from all eternity did, by the most wise and holy counsel of his own will, freely and unchangeably ordain whatsoever comes to pass: yet so, as thereby neither is God the author of sin, nor is violence offered to the will of the creatures, nor is the liberty or contingency of second causes taken away, but rather established.

II. Although God knows whatsoever may or can come to pass upon all supposed conditions; yet hath he not decreed anything because he foresaw it as future, or as that which would come to pass upon such conditions.

III. By the decree of God, for the manifestation of his glory, some men and angels are predestinated unto everlasting life, and others foreordained to everlasting death.

IV. These angels and men, thus predestinated and foreordained, are particularly and unchangeably designed; and their number is so certain and definite, that it cannot be either increased or diminished.

V. Those of mankind that are predestinated unto life, God, before the foundation of the world was laid, according to his eternal and immutable purpose, and the secret counsel and good pleasure of his will, hath chosen in Christ unto everlasting glory, out of his mere free grace and love, without any foresight of faith or good works, or perseverance in either of them, or any other thing in the creature, as conditions, or causes moving him thereunto; and all to the praise of his glorious grace.

VI. As God hath appointed the elect unto glory, so hath he, by the eternal and most free purpose of his will, foreordained all the means thereunto. Wherefore they who are elected being fallen in Adam, are redeemed by Christ; are effectually called unto faith in Christ by his Spirit working in due season; are justified, adopted, sanctified, and kept by his power through faith unto salvation. Neither are any other redeemed by Christ, effectually called, justified, adopted, sanctified, and saved, but the elect only.

VII. The rest of mankind, God was pleased, according to the unsearchable counsel of his own will, whereby he extendeth or withholdeth mercy as he pleaseth, for the glory of his sovereign power over his creatures, to pass by, and to ordain them to dishonour and wrath for their sin, to the praise of his glorious justice.

VIII. The doctrine of this high mystery of predestination is to be handled with special prudence and care, that men attending the will of God revealed in his word, and yielding obedience thereunto, may, from the certainty of their effectual vocation, be assured of their eternal election. So shall this doctrine afford matter of praise, reverence, and admiration of God, and of humility, diligence, and abundant consolation, to all that sincerely obey the Gospel.

Chapter IX—*Of Free Will*

I. God hath endued the will of man with that natural liberty, that it is neither forced, nor by any absolute necessity of nature determined, to good or evil.

II. Man, in his state of innocency, had freedom and power to will and to do that which is good and well-pleasing to God; but yet mutably, so that he might fall from it.

III. Man, by his fall into a state of sin, hath wholly lost all ability of will to any spiritual good accompanying salvation; so as a natural man, being altogether averse from that good, and dead in sin, is not able, by his own strength, to convert himself, or to prepare himself thereunto.

IV. When God converts a sinner, and translates him into the state of grace, he freeth him from his natural bondage under sin, and by his grace alone enables him freely to will and to do that which is spiritually good; yet so as that, by reason of his remaining corruption, he doth not perfectly nor only will that which is good, but doth also will that which is evil.

V. The will of man is made perfectly and immutably free to do good alone in the state of glory only.

Chapter X—*Of Effectual Calling*

I. All those whom God hath predestinated unto life, and those only, he is pleased, in his appointed and accepted time, effectually to call, by his word and Spirit, out of that state of sin and death in which they are by nature, to grace and salvation by Jesus Christ; enlightening their minds spiritually and savingly to understand the things of God; taking away their heart of stone, and giving unto them an heart of flesh; renewing their wills, and by his almighty power determining them to that which is good; and effectually drawing them to Jesus Christ; yet so as they come most freely, being made willing by his grace.

II. This effectual call is of God's free and special grace alone, not from any thing at all foreseen in man; who is altogether passive therein, until, being quickened and renewed by the Holy Spirit, he is thereby enabled to answer this call, and to embrace the grace offered and conveyed in it.

III. Elect infants, dying in infancy, are regenerated and saved by Christ through the Spirit, who worketh when, and where, and how he pleaseth. So also are all other elect persons, who are incapable of being outwardly called by the ministry of the word.

IV. Others not elected, although they may be called by the ministry of the word, and may have some common operations of the Spirit, yet they never truly come unto Christ, and therefore cannot be saved: much less can men not professing the Christian religion be saved in any other way whatsoever, be they ever so diligent to frame their lives according to the light of nature, and the law of that religion they do profess; and to assert and maintain that they may, is very pernicious, and to be detested.

Westminster Confession of Faith, 1646

Reformed

XV. *Of Original Sin*

We believe that, through the disobedience of Adam, original sin is extended to all mankind; which is a corruption of the whole nature, and an hereditary disease, wherewith infants themselves are infected even in their mother's womb, and which produceth in man all sorts of sin, being in him as a root thereof; and therefore is so vile and abominable in the sight of God, that it is sufficient to condemn all mankind. Nor is it by any means abolished or done away by baptism; since sin always issues forth from this woeful source, as water from a fountain; notwithstanding it is not imputed to the children of God unto condemnation, but by his grace and mercy is forgiven them. Not that they should rest securely in sin, but that a sense of this corruption should make believers often to sigh, desiring to be delivered from this body of death. Wherefore we reject the error of the Pelagians, who assert that sin proceeds only from imitation.

XVI. *Of Eternal Election*

We believe that all the posterity of Adam being thus fallen into perdition and ruin, by the sin of our first parents, God then did manifest himself such as he is; that is to say, merciful and just: Merciful, since he delivers and preserves from this perdition all, whom he, in his eternal and unchangeable counsel of mere goodness, hath elected in Christ Jesus our Lord, without any respect to their works: Just, in leaving others in the fall and perdition wherein they have involved themselves.

The Belgic Confession, 1561

Recommended Reading
(an asterisk marks outstanding works)

*Boettner, Loraine. *The Reformed Doctrine of Predestination*. Philadelphia: Presbyterian and Reformed, (1932) 1963.

Boyce, James P. *Abstract of Systematic Theology* (1887). North Pompano Baptist Church, 1101 N.E. 33rd St., Pompano Beach, FL 33064. (50% discount if you mention *75 Bible Questions*.)

Calvin, John. *Concerning the Eternal Predestination of God*. London: James Clarke & Co., 1961.

Cheeseman, John, *et al*. *The Grace of God in the Gospel*. London: Banner of Truth, 1972.

*Clark, Gordon H. *Biblical Predestination*. Nutley, NJ: Presbyterian and Reformed, 1969.

Girardeau, John. *Calvinism and Evangelical Arminianism*. Box 1094, Harrisonburg, VA: Sprinkle Publications, 1984.

Gill, John. *The Cause of God and Truth*. Grand Rapids: Sovereign Grace Publishers, 1971. (Baptist theologian, late 17th century)

Haldane, Robert. *An Exposition of the Epistle to the Romans*. Reprint edition; Marshallton, DE: National Foundation for Christian Education, 1970. (early 19th century)

Hodge, Charles. *Commentary on the Epistle to the Romans*. Reprint edition; Grand Rapids: Eerdmans, 1950. (late 19th century)

Kuyper, Abraham. *Lectures on Calvinism*. Grand Rapids: Eerdmans, (1898) 1931.

*Luther, Martin. *The Bondage of the Will*. Westwood, NJ: Fleming H. Revell, (1525) 1957.

Mell, P. H. *A Southern Baptist Looks at Predestination.* (late 19th century). North Pompano Baptist Church. (50% discount if you mention *75 Bible Questions*.)

*Murray, John. *The Epistle to the Romans*. Grand Rapids: Eerdmans, 1965.

_____ . *The Imputation of Adam's Sin*. Nutley, NJ: Presbyterian and Reformed, 1977.

_____ . *Redemption—Accomplished and Applied*. Grand Rapids: Eerdmans, 1955.

North, Gary. *Unconditional Surrender: God's Program for Victory*. 3rd edition; Ft. Worth, Texas: Dominion Press, 1988, Part I.

Owen, John. *The Death of Death in the Death of Christ*. Reprint edition; London: Banner of Truth, 1959. (mid-17th century)

Packer, J. I. *Evangelism and the Sovereignty of God*. Chicago: InterVarsity Press, 1961. (Anglican theologian)

Pink, Arthur. *The Sovereignty of God*. London: Banner of Truth, 1961. (Baptist theologian)

Robertson, Norvelle. *Church Members' Handbook of Theology*. Box 1094, Harrisonburg, VA: Sprinkle Pubs., (1874). (Southern Baptist theologian)

Shedd, W. G. T. *Dogmatic Theology*. Reprint edition; Nashville: Thomas Nelson Sons. (late 19th century)

*Steele, David N., and Curtis C. Thomas. *The Five Points of Calvinism: Defined, Defended, Documented*. Phillipsburg, NJ: Presbyterian and Reformed, 1963.

Van Til, Cornelius. *Christianity and Barthianism*. Philadelphia: Presbyterian and Reformed, 1962.

_____ . *A Christian Theory of Knowledge*. Philadelphia: Presbyterian and Reformed, 1969.

_____ . *The Defense of the Faith*. Philadelphia: Presbyterian and Reformed, 1967.

_____ . *An Introduction to Systematic Theology*. Phillipsburg, NJ: Presbyterian and Reformed, 1978.

_____ . *Psychology of Religion*. Phillipsburg, NJ: Presbyterian and Reformed, 1971.

Warfield, Benjamin B. *Calvin and Augustine*. Reprint edition; Philadelphia: Presbyterian and Reformed, (1932) 1956.

_____ . *The Plan of Salvation*. Reprint edition; Grand Rapids: Eerdmans, 1955.

Part II
LAW: GOD'S OR MAN'S

Introduction to Part II

The question of the law of God has been controversial in Protestant circles for over a century. Most churches today believe that the laws found in the Old Testament are no longer binding. This has not always been the belief of Christians. The Puritans of New England established their colonies specifically in terms of their belief in the continuing validity of the laws of God. Certainly, Christians have affirmed their faith in the so-called *moral* laws of God. But in the late nineteenth century, in certain fundamentalist circles, people began to abandon any faith in the continuing validity of Old Testament law. In fact, many prominent pastors and theologians have actually said that it is illegitimate to preach the Ten Commandments in New Testament times. One such pastor was the Presbyterian leader of the 1950's, Donald J. Barnhouse.

Does the New Testament teach such a doctrine of law? Does the New Testament abandon Old Testament law? That's what this section of the book deals with.

Let me ask you a question. When you hear the words, "the *principles* of the Bible," or "the *moral teachings* of the Bible," don't you instinctively think to yourself, "the *laws* of the Bible"? If the principles are binding, aren't they laws? A lot of Christian teachers are "fudging" by switching words on you. They claim that "we're not under the law," yet they try to take a stand against immorality by proclaiming the validity of a group of biblical *principles*. But what specifically *are* these principles? Where do we find them, if not in the Bible? How can we even define "immorality" if we reject the idea that God's laws are still binding?

If we reject God's definitions of immorality, haven't we thereby become *humanists*, inventing our own definitions of immoral behavior? Isn't one of the most important aspects of secular humanism the attempt to substitute man's laws for God's laws? In short, how can anyone successfully fight secular humanism if he already accepts the premise of humanism's ethics, namely, that the laws of the God of the Old Testament are no longer binding?

I propose the following principle of biblical interpretation (or hermeneutic) because I believe it was the one which Paul adopted in his epistles. First, we must assert that all the revealed laws of God are always binding *in principle*, for they reflect His unchanging moral character. Second, we must admit that the *applications* of some of God's laws have been changed by God as a result of Christ's death and resurrection. For example, the moral necessity of a blood covering for sin is always binding, but we no longer sacrifice animals, because Christ's sacrifice is behind us historically. Third, we must affirm that *unless* the New Testament explicitly announces that the *former application* of a *still morally binding* law has been changed by God, we should still honor it in its Old Testament details. If you disagree with this approach, consider the following 25 questions.

The very first question is "hard core." It will shock some people. But it gets my point across early: if the New Testament is the Christian's only guide for moral behavior, we are in big trouble morally. We need the Old Testament, too.

Question 26
Isn't It Immoral for People to Have Sex with Animals?

Neither shalt thou lie with any beast to defile thyself therewith: neither shall any woman stand before a beast to lie down thereto: it is confusion (Leviticus 18:23).

What Christian wouldn't affirm the immorality of such an act? Why even include it in this book? Simple: the New Testament doesn't mention bestiality. It's an Old Testament prohibition. So the question now arises: Is Old Testament law still morally and legally binding on church members?

There are many Christians who say that Old Testament laws no longer apply to Christians unless the New Testament reaffirmed a particular Old Testament law. But the New Testament doesn't mention this Old Testament prohibition. Are we to conclude that this issue is morally an "open question"? But God says that bestiality requires the death penalty: **"Whosoever lieth with a beast shall surely be put to death"** (Ex. 22:19).

On the other hand, if we accept the principle of biblical interpretation that all Old Testament laws are still completely binding on Christians unless a New Testament passage has released us from the obligation, then we can say in confidence that such an act is an "abomination." **"Defile not ye yourselves in any of these things: for in all these the nations are defiled which I cast out before you: And the land is defiled: therefore I do visit the iniquity thereof upon it, and the land itself vomiteth out her inhabitants"** (Leviticus 18:24-25).

Questionable Answer

"Everyone knows that such an act is immoral. The New Testament writers assumed that Christians would know this. The light of redeemed wisdom shows this to all Christians. The Spirit would not lead Christians to do such things. We are morally bound, not legally bound, to obey such a prohibition."

My Reply: Are we bound to obey this law because it is a universally recognized evil practice? It certainly was not recognized as evil by the Canaanites. And if Christians should gain political influence, shouldn't they make such practices illegal, so as not to have the land vomit out an entire population?

Are we bound by this law? If so, why? Because it is "logical"? Logical for whom? *By what standard?* Or because "all righteous men know not to practice such acts"? But how can we measure righteousness apart from the prohibition?

If we are bound by this law, then why are we supposedly not bound by all Old Testament laws? What about marrying your sister or brother, or an aunt or uncle? The Old Testament prohibits such marriages (Leviticus 18:6-18); the New Testament doesn't. If God's word isn't authoritative, both Old and New Testaments, then what is? The temporary morality of some temporary nation or church? The temporary morality of mankind? How can we understand right and wrong if we exclude the Old Testament's legal precepts? How can we avoid humanism's "situation ethics"? How can our nation avoid God's judgment?

For further study: Lev. 22:31-33; Matt. 5:17-20; 23:23; Rom. 8:3-4.

Question 27

How Can We Love God but Ignore God's Law?

And hereby we do know that we know him, if we keep his commandments. He that saith, I know him, and keepeth not his commandments, is a liar, and the truth is not in him. But whoso keepeth his word, in him verily is the love of God perfected: hereby know we that we are in him (I John 2:3-5).

The problem that John was dealing with was *self-knowledge*. How does a Christian know if he really is "in Christ" as a redeemed person? John's answer is *the law of God*. It is not emotionalism, or a one-time profession of faith, or the ability to speak in an unknown tongue, or the ability to cast out demons in the name of Jesus. It is our adherence to the commandments of Christ.

The question will come up: Are Christ's commandments different from Old Testament laws? To answer this crucial question, we need to ask ourselves some preliminary questions. First, is there an *ethical* difference between God the Father and God the Son? Second, did Christ subordinate His will to His Father's will? Third, is the ethical condition of sinful men or redeemed men different in principle in New Testament times than in Old Testament times? Fourth, are the ethical problems faced by people today fundamentally different from those faced by Old Testament people? Fifth, are the social and economic problems fundamentally different? (The numbers are no doubt larger—more people, larger cities, more wealth—but are the issues different?)

Questionable Answer

"The death and resurrection of Christ released men from the bondage of Old Testament law. Old Testament statutes are a dead letter today. Only those laws announced by Christ and the New Testament authors are morally binding, let alone binding in terms of civil law."

My Reply: Why did the New Testament authors, especially John but also Paul, continue to return to the theme of *God's commandments* as *ethical indicators?* Why did they point to each man's need for a standard of evaluation for his spiritual condition? Why did they believe that one's ethical standing before God is reflected by his outward performance of God's commandments? Why did Christ and John especially argue that *inward life* is to be judged by *outward conformity to God's law?* Where do we find God's law?

They understood that what a man *does* is in close conformity to what he **really** *believes*. Christ criticized the Pharisees for not giving their parents money, because they said they needed to give it to God. **"Thus have ye made the commandment of God of none effect by your tradition"** (Matthew 15:6). **"Woe unto you, scribes and Pharisees, hypocrites! For ye pay tithe of mint and anise and cummin, and have omitted the weightier matters of the law: judgment, mercy, and faith; these ought ye to have done, and not to leave the other undone"** (Matthew 23:23). He criticized their *hypocrisy*, not Old Testament law.

For further study: Ex. 20:6; Deut. 6:5; 7:9; 10:12; Dan. 9:4; Matt. 22:37; John 14:15, 21; I John 5:3.

Question 28

Is Profession of Faith Enough, or Do Our Acts Also Count?

Not every one that saith unto me, Lord, Lord, shall enter into the kingdom of heaven; but he that doeth the will of my Father which is in heaven (Matthew 7:21).

"Taking the Lord's name in vain" is not just cursing. It is also the *unbeliever's* proclaiming of God's name while performing works that impress men but not God. The Pharisees gave charity in public so that all men could see them. **"They have their reward,"** Christ said sarcastically—their prestige among men, but also final judgment. Seven sons of Sceva tried to cast out demons in Jesus' name, and a demon leaped upon them and drove them out of the house, naked and bruised (Acts 19:13-17).

Jesus knew what spiritual impostors would do. **"Many will say to me in that day, Lord, Lord, have we not prophesied in thy name and in thy name have cast out devils? And in thy name done many wonderful works? And then will I profess unto them, I never knew you: depart from me, ye that work iniquity"** (Matthew 7:22-23).

How can a person test himself, or anyone else, to determine whether he is a spiritual counterfeit? **"Beware of false prophets, which come to you in sheep's clothing, but inwardly they are ravening wolves. Ye shall know them by their fruits. Do men gather grapes of thorns, or figs of thistles? Even so every good tree bringeth forth good fruit; but a corrupt tree bringeth forth evil fruit"** (Matthew 7:15-17).

Questionable Answer

"Jesus was speaking of spiritual gifts of the Spirit, not the details of Old Testament law. Without love and charity, and a willingness to forgive men, all men's works mean nothing (I Corinthians 13)."

My Reply: But what are "spiritual gifts"? They are not exclusively invisible gifts, because Christ spoke of *visible fruits*. They are *acts* that can be evaluated by a standard. The question is: *By what standard?*

In contrast to gifts of the spirit are *evil fruit*. Evil acts are called **"the works of the flesh"** by Paul. What are they? **"Now the works of the flesh are manifest, which are these: adultery, fornication, uncleanness, lasciviousness, idolatry, witchcraft, hatred, variance [quarrels], emulations [jealousy], wrath, strife, seditions [intrigues], heresies, envyings, murders, drunkenness, revellings, and such like"** (Galatians 5:19-21a). These are acts of *lawlessness.*

"But the fruit of the Spirit is love, joy, peace, long-suffering, gentleness, goodness, faith, meekness, temperance: against such there is no law" (Galatians 5:22-23). This implies that there *is* a law against the other acts—not necessarily civil law, but God's law. The specific nature of evil acts makes Paul's point clear: do these, and you do not enter heaven (5:21b). Thus, *our standard of ethical evaluation is God's law.* As Christ warned: *"Beware of false prophets."* They will teach you to pay no attention to God's law.

For further study: Ps. 19:7-11; 119:105, 129-30; Prov. 6:23; Isa. 8:20.

Question 29
If Men Won't Obey God's Law, Are They Saved?

They profess that they know God; but in works they deny him, being abominable, and disobedient, and unto every good work reprobate (Titus 1:16).

Reprobation is normally discussed in terms of a denial of faith in Jesus Christ's divinity, death, resurrection, second coming, and eternal Lordship. A reprobate person is someone who denies the necessity of a substitutionary atonement to God for sin. Yet Paul here links reprobation and lawlessness. A man who does evil works testifies to his condition as an ethical rebel who does not love God and who has not been regenerated by God's grace. *Doing evil works is equivalent to denying Jesus Christ*. Yet these reprobate men professed Christ verbally.

In Revelation 3:1, we read: **"And unto the angel of the church in Sardis write: These things saith he that hath the seven Spirits of God, and the seven stars; I know thy works, that thou hast a name that thou livest [a name for being alive], and art dead."** This is New Testament doctrine.

Ezekiel cried out to God in opposition to the Israelites of his day: **"And they come unto thee as the people cometh, and they sit before thee as my people, and they hear thy words, but they will not do them: for with their mouth they shew much love, but their heart goeth after their covetousness"** (33:31). A true profession of faith is what you *say* and *do*, not just what you *say*. Your way of life must conform to your confession.

Questionable Answer

"All this talk about doing good works is misleading. Paul says over and over that we are justified by faith, not works. What saves a man is his profession of faith, not doing good works."

My Reply: James said: **"Even so faith, if it hath not works, is dead, being alone. Yea, a man may say, Thou hast faith, and I have works: Show me thy faith without thy works, and I will show thee my faith by my works. Thou believest that there is one God; thou doest well: the devils also believe, and tremble. But wilt thou know, O vain man, that faith without works is dead?"** (James 2:17-20).

How could anything be more clear? Faith is not merely a set of intellectual beliefs concerning the nature of God. Devils know there is one God, yet they are destined for eternal punishment. So are verbally professing, evil-doing Church members, he implies. *Faith is a **way of life**—a way of life which has outward manifestations in men's **actions***. James made it clear: he judged men by their works, for works testify to the specific character of their faith. In short, *a valid profession of faith cannot be separated from Bible-based, Bible-judged works*.

Redemption is ethical. Ethics and faith are inescapably related. If what a man does denies what he says, what he does constitutes his profession of faith. His acts reveal his god. Your acts testify to your God, too. *By what standard* do you judge the legitimacy of your acts?

For further study: II Cor. 5:15; Titus 2:14; 3:8; Jas. 2:14-26.

Question 30
Are We "Once Saved, Always Saved"?

> They went out from us, but they were not of us; for if they had been of us, they would no doubt have continued with us: but they went out, that they might be made manifest that they were not all of us (I John 2:19).

The test of whether a person stands with Christ or is self-deluded is his *perseverance in the faith*. People are sometimes self-deluded about their Christian faith. Paul spoke of Hymenaeus and Alexander, whose faith was "made shipwreck" (I Timothy 1:19-20). He mentions Hymenaeus again as a heretic (II Timothy 2:17). Demas was Paul's fellow laborer (Philemon 24). But Paul later spoke of Demas as a man who **"hath forsaken me, having loved this present world, and is departed unto Thessalonica"** (II Timothy 4:10). He only *thought* he was saved.

A famous passage dealing with people who once profess faith in Christ but who later reject the faith is Jesus' parable of the four soils: wayside, stony ground, thorny soil, and good soil. Only the good soil produced permanent abundance (Matthew 13:3-8). The message was the same: the gospel of the kingdom of God. Those who hear the message don't respond in the same way. In the case of the wayside, the man doesn't respond at all. In the next two cases, men respond temporarily, and then their (non-saving) faith dies (Matt 13:19-23). Yet in these latter cases, there was an initial commitment, until things got hot or full of cares (the deceitfulness of riches: v. 22).

Questionable Answer

"The Bible is clear: once you make a profession of faith, God honors that profession (Romans 10:9-10). If a man makes that profession of faith in Christ, he is forever sealed by the Holy Spirit."

My Reply: Paul wrote in Romans 10 that we must *confess* Christ and believe in our hearts that God has raised Him from the dead. Problem: What if we *cease* to confess Him or to believe that God has raised Him from the dead? What if by our public acts of sin or our public confession of faith, we *renounce Christ and His gospel?* Then the promise no longer applies. We never possessed true saving faith.

"Once saved, always saved" is quite correct. But is "saved" the same as "I made a confession of faith 23 years ago, when I was young and foolish, and which I no longer believe"? Some expositors argue erroneously that "Once confessed, always possessed." There is nothing in the Bible that supports this interpretation. Demas once confessed. So did Hymenaeus. It did them no good. In fact, it did them worse harm, for they had been given much, and **"unto whomsoever much is given, of him shall be much required"** (Luke 12:48b). Men sometimes change their confessions.

How do we know if we still believe in Christ? Jesus said: **"He that hath my commandments, and keepeth them, he it is that loveth me"** (John 14:21a). *We test our faith by His commandments.*

For further study: John 15:10; Phil. 2:12-13; Col. 1:22-23; Heb. 3:12-14; 6:4-12; 10:26-39; I John 2:3-4.

Question 31
How Can We Accurately Define Sin if We Deny God's Law?

Whosoever committeth sin transgresseth also the law: for sin is the transgression of the law (I John 3:4).

It is unlikely that any Christian wants to argue that the New Testament writers wanted to promote sin. Throughout the Bible, the warning against sinful thoughts and behavior is repeated, from Genesis to Revelation. But the question inevitably arises: What exactly constitutes sin? The first epistle of John focuses on this question. Few sermons are preached from this epistle.

At the center of any biblical discussion about *sin* is the issue of *biblical law*. (As a matter of fact, at the very center of discussion of the foundations of any civilization is the question of some form of law.) What is the relationship between the biblical definition of sin and biblical law?

Men are to do good works and shun evil works. But how are Christians supposed to define sin? How are they to discover which act or thought is sinful, and which is good? James said: **"Therefore to him that knoweth to do good, and doeth it not, to him it is sin"** (James 4:17). But this still doesn't answer the question: What is good? *By what standard do we determine what is good?*

What other answer can there be for a Christian? *Our standard is biblical law.* Where else can we go to find a valid standard? To human logic? To antichristian religions? To our own feelings? Why look anywhere else but in the Old and New Testaments?

Questionable Answer

"To attempt to enforce biblical law on people would involve setting up a theocracy. We all know what *that* means! It would be a tyranny. We are under grace, not law."

My Reply: On the contrary, *we are under some other god's civil law*. Christ made this plain: *there is no neutrality*. Law is an *inescapable concept*. It is never a question of "law vs. no law"; it is a question of *whose* law. This is why Christ said: **"Take my yoke upon you, and learn of me; for I am meek and lowly in heart: and ye shall find rest unto your souls. For my yoke is easy, and my burden is light"** (Matthew 11:29-30). Christ never offered His followers a world without a yoke. No such world exists. He offered His people a better yoke, a lighter yoke. If we don't bear Christ's yoke, we bear Satan's yoke.

Christ challenged the traditional, legalistic interpretations of the Pharisees and scribes. He said: **"For they bind heavy burdens and grievous to be borne, and lay them on men's shoulders; but they themselves will not move them with one of their fingers"** (Matthew 23:4). But Christ *never* challenged the validity of Old Testament law. After all, He wrote it! In contrast to the *traditional, humanistic law of the Pharisees* stands God's law. **"For this is the love of God, that we keep his commandments: and his commandments are not grievous"** (I John 5:3). Has anyone taught you that God's laws *are* in some way grievous?

For further study: Ps. 119:2-3, 9-11; Isa. 51:7; Dan. 9:11; Mark 7:1-23.

Question 32
Does God Answer Prayers of Lawbreakers?

And whatsoever we ask, we receive of him, because we keep his commandments, and do those things that are pleasing in his sight (I John 3:22).

A Christian's prayer life is a very important aspect of his daily walk with God. Even if he ignores it, it is nonetheless very important. So it is understandable that Christians should look to the Bible in order to discover what God has to say about prayer. What He says is not always discussed by Bible teachers.

Consider the words of Solomon: **"He that turneth away his ear from hearing the law, even his prayer shall be abomination"** (Proverbs 28:9). Does this mean that people who violate biblical law cannot get their prayers heard by God? He knows when men pray; physically He is not deaf. But He turns a "deaf ear" to all such prayers. **"If I regard iniquity in my heart, the LORD will not hear me"** (Psalm 66:18). God *ignores* such prayers.

Sacrifices in the Old Testament were a form of prayer: a cry unto God to forgive men for their sins. But sacrifices without obedience were like prayer without obedience. God did not respect them. **"Hath the LORD as great delight in burnt offerings and sacrifices, as in obeying the voice of the LORD? Behold, to obey is better than sacrifice, and to hearken than the fat of rams"** (I Samuel 15:22). In short, **"The sacrifice of the wicked is an abomination to the LORD"** (Proverbs 15:8). God stated this repeatedly (Jeremiah 7:22-23; Micah 6:6-8).

Questionable Answer

"It is ridiculous to argue that God doesn't hear the prayer of a Christian who no longer obeys the laws of the Old Testament. We no longer offer bulls and rams to placate God. Those laws don't apply any longer. Neither do the civil laws of Israel. God hears our prayers, and has for 2,000 years."

My Reply: The *outward manifestation* of *some* of the Old Testament laws no longer are the same. We do not sacrifice animals. But the epistle to the Hebrews makes it clear why we don't: the Old Testament sacrificial system had pointed to Christ's final sacrifice, so it is no longer binding. But sacrifice is still binding: Christ's, and then our own personal, living sacrifice (Romans 12:1). God did not abolish sacrifice; He replaced a *temporary* sacrificial ritual.

Does God answer prayers of Christians who categorically reject the doctrine of the binding nature of all Old Testament laws that *have not been explicitly restated in the New Testament?* Yes, He does. But doesn't this deny the teaching of the Bible? Not at all. Jesus Christ intercedes for us constantly before the throne of God (Romans 8:33-34). So does the Holy Spirit (Romans 8:26). Jesus Christ fulfilled all the terms of God's law (Matthew 5:17-18), so God honors His intercessory prayers on our behalf, even if we sinfully fail to obey His laws. Does this mean we should now sin with abandon? God forbid! (Romans 6:1-2).

So, if you want more of your prayers answered, start obeying God's laws.

For further study: Prov. 15:29; 21:27; Isa. 1:10-15; Amos 5:21-24; John 9:31; Jas. 4:3.

Question 33

Do We Really Love the Brethren if We Disobey God's Laws?

Whosoever believeth that Jesus is the Christ is born of God: and every one that loveth him that begat loveth him also that is begotten of him. By this we know that we love the children of God, when we love God, and keep his commandments (I John 5:1-2).

John's argument is not instantly clear. We have to think about what he is saying. First, if we believe in Jesus, we are born of God. But how do we know if we *really* believe in Jesus—believe in Him in a saving sense? Because we are born (meaning born again, or born from above [John 3:3]) by God. Third, others are born by God. Fourth, we must love the children of God as brothers if we are to consider ourselves as adopted (ethical, regenerate) sons of God.

But what does "love" mean? Warm feelings? Sometimes. A personal closeness to others? Sometimes. Trust in others? Sometimes. But what must it *always* mean? What is love's *defining characteristic*? John tells us: *keeping God's commandments.*

Paul tells us much the same thing. **"Owe no man any thing, but to love one another: for he that loveth another hath fulfilled the law"** (Romans 13:8). Paul meant that if we do our best to regard the other person's best interests, we have fulfilled the law. But how do we know his best interests? *By what standard* can we properly evaluate those interests? We are back to the issue of *biblical law*. If this isn't our standard, what is?

Questionable Answer

"Loving the other person means to have a right relationship with that person. It has nothing to do with biblical law, if you mean Old Testament law. Personal relationships are what count, not the killing details of Old Testament law."

My Reply: If Old Testament law was so "killingly restrictive," consider Romans 13:8. It forbids *all* personal debt. But Deuteronomy 15 allowed at least a 7-year emergency debt. So which is more rigorous? (And is the critic 100% out of personal debt?)

Personal relationships were just as important in the Old Testament era as they are today. That is *why* God gave His law. God gave Old Testament believers biblical law in order to reduce outward sin, thereby reducing disputes. Old Testament law also reminded men of inward sin, and their own lack of personal merit—the need for a substitutionary blood sacrifice.

The important fact to observe is Paul's explanation of what "love as the fulfilling of the law" means. It means Old Testament law: "**For this, Thou shalt not commit adultery, Thou shalt not kill, Thou shalt not steal, Thou shalt not bear false witness, Thou shalt not covet; and if there be any other commandment, it is briefly comprehended in this saying, namely, Thou shalt love thy neighbor as thyself. Love worketh no ill to his neighbour: therefore love is the fulfilling of the law**" (Romans 13:9-10). If you really love your Christian brethren, will you deliberately violate God's laws regarding personal relationships?

For further study: Lev. 19:18; Matt. 22:39; John 13:34-35; Gal. 5:14; Jas. 2:8; I John 4:20-21.

Question 34
How Can We Identify Christians if We Ignore God's Law?

> In this the children of God are manifest, and the children of the devil: whosoever doeth not righteousness is not of God, neither he that loveth not his brother (I John 3:10).

The doing of righteousness and the loving of the Christian brother are inseparably linked by John. We can identify Christians and Satanists by means of God's standards of righteousness.

Two questions immediately come to mind. First, what are the specific details of righteousness, by which we can identify other Christians? Second, what is the meaning of "loving the brother"?

We have already surveyed the meaning of biblical love. It means doing righteously, in terms of the specifics of biblical law (Question 33). Thus, when John directs our attention to *righteousness* as the identifying characteristic of the Christian, he is directing our attention to *biblical law*.

Sometimes righteousness doesn't involve relationships with Christian brothers. Does this destroy the meaning of John's message? Not at all. Doing righteously means doing unto others as we would have them do unto us. This same rule governs *all* our relationships with other men, Christian and non-Christian. So "doing righteousness" means honoring the specifics of God's law. If we fail to honor His law, then we are separating ourselves from the family of God. We are identifying with Satan.

Questionable Answer

"Christians are led by the Holy Spirit. The Spirit personally guides them in all their relationships with other men, believers and non-believers. This leadership of the Holy Spirit is crucial. He is the source of righteousness and love. Old Testament law has nothing to do with the leading of the Spirit."

My Reply: "**Beloved, believe not every spirit, but try the spirits whether they are of God: because many false prophets are gone out into the world**" (I John 4:1). This is the heart of the matter. We must try the spirits.

How do we "try the spirits"? How do we know that it was the Holy Spirit who spoke? There are other spirits —familiar spirits, the Old Testament calls them—that whisper in the minds of men. We test the spirits in the same way that we test prophets: *by the law of God.* In Deuteronomy 13, God warns men not to listen to any prophet, dreamer of dreams, or worker of signs if he calls the people of God to worship a different God (13:1-3). Immediately thereafter, we read: "**Ye shall walk after the LORD your God, and fear him, and keep his commandments, and obey his voice, and ye shall serve him, and cleave unto him. And that prophet, or that dreamer of dreams, shall be put to death; because he hath spoken to turn you away from the LORD**" (13:4-5a). We use God's law to test the spirits. If we abandon God's law, how will we test what we think is the Spirit's guidance? God's Holy Spirit doesn't tell us to disobey God's holy law. But unholy men do.

For further study: Ex. 19:5-6; Ps. 1:2; 40:8; 119:35, 47, 72, 92, 97; Jer. 31:33; Heb. 8:10; Rev. 22:14.

Question 35

How Can We Know if We Are "Dead to Sin" if We Ignore God's Law?

What shall we say then? Shall we continue in sin, that grace may abound? God forbid. How shall we, that are dead to sin, live any longer therein? (Romans 6:1-2).

Paul argues in Romans 5 that by the sin of one man, Adam, sin entered the world, and death by this sin (v. 12). Without law, sin is not imputed to man (13), Paul says, but since death reigned from Adam until Moses (14), we know that the law existed and was binding. God gave men the law, that man's offense "might abound," and therefore that the grace of God might abound even more (20). In other words, the law points out the deadly nature of our sin. Our sin is in every area of life, in the whole fabric of our being. God's law is therefore comprehensive, in order to reveal to us just exactly how evil we are in *all* areas of life.

Should we sin therefore that grace might abound? No! Christians are *dead* to sin. The *knowledge* of sin killed Paul, he says, and it was the law that brought him this necessary knowledge (Romans 7:9-11). Christ then raised him from the dead.

We dare not live in sin, he says (6:2). But how do we know when we are *living* in sin? The same way we knew, as unregenerate people, that we were *dying* in sin before: *by God's law*. We are *dead to sin* because we can now *escape its deadly effects*.

Questionable Answer

"By returning to a fear of Old Testament law, we place ourselves under the bondage of law. Law is to reveal sin to us, in order that we might trust Christ. Once we trust Him, we are released from any requirement to obey Old Testament law."

My Reply: Biblical law creates fear of God's final judgment in those who are perishing. It is not designed to create this kind of fear in the regenerate. We are dead to sin through Christ's grace. We cannot die the "second death" of eternal punishment (Revelation 20:14). So the law of God has no terrors for us!

The law is an *ethical spotlight*. It reveals the dark deeds of evil men, who prefer light to darkness (John 3:19). But it is no threat to Christ's redeemed, for it is this spotlight which enables us to walk the path of righteousness. Like the speed limit that is a threat to speeders and reckless drivers, but a source of safety to other drivers and pedestrians, so is biblical law. We should obey the speed limits because we are good drivers who care about everyone's safety, including our own. So should we obey the law of God.

Would critics of biblical law also encourage us to drive as fast as we can, whenever we choose? If not, then why do they tell us to ignore the specifics of biblical law? *How can we live ethically without God's ethical guidelines?* Doesn't God's law function analogously to the speed limit, to protect us and those around us? Should we reject protection?

For further study: Deut. 4:1-2; 12:32; Ps. 37:30-31; Eccl. 12:13-14; I Cor. 6:9-11; Gal. 5:19-21.

Question 36

How Can We "Walk in Newness of Life" if We Disobey God's Law?

Therefore we are buried with him by baptism into death: that like as Christ was raised up from the dead by the glory of the Father, even so we also should walk in newness of life (Romans 6:4).

It is our spiritual death with Christ in baptism which makes us dead to sin. Sin kills, by means of the law. There is no escape from death for man. He either dies *eternally* as a result of sin's effects on his life, or else the old unethical Adam dies in Christ's death. *Death is an inescapable concept*. There is no way to escape this effect of Adam's transgression. God told Adam he would surely die if he rebelled. God did not lie; Satan lied when he denied God's warning. We are *born ethically dead*. The consequences of this "physically living death" are our eventual physical death and eternal judgment.

The **"newness of life"** referred to by Paul is *ethical regeneration*. We live ethically acceptable lives before God now, for God looks at the life of His Son and imputes (judicially declares) Christ's righteousness to us. So we can walk before God as living creatures who are not doomed to eternal destruction.

Should we walk as before, pretending that this world isn't governed by God's law, pretending that we were ethically alive in our own sinful autonomy, content to act as we pleased? No. We should walk in the paths of righteousness. Question: How do we know what path this is at any point in time? *God's law!*

Questionable Answer

"The words 'newness of life' refer to a life no longer governed by concerns about the specific details of Old Testament law. Old Testament law has nothing to do with Christ's commandments. We walk free because we walk without concern over God's law."

My Reply: We walk free without fear of eternal death which resulted from our sin, and was *revealed* to us by God's law. But does this mean that we walk free because we no longer need to conform our thoughts and behavior to the requirements of God's law? On the contrary, *we walk free because God's law is in our hearts,* and we progressively discipline ourselves to the requirements of God's law, making our righteous behavior more and more automatic.

This is New Testament doctrine. Citing Jeremiah 31:33, the author of Hebrews wrote: **"For this is the covenant that I will make with the house of Israel after those days, saith the Lord; I will put my laws into their mind, and write them in their hearts: and I will be to them a God, and they shall be to me a people"** (Hebrews 8:10). He was so concerned that we understand that this prophecy is fulfilled in the church age that he repeated it a few paragraphs later (10:16). It is not that the law is *over* us like some frightful sword; the law is *in* us, as our very conscience. Yet there are Bible teachers who insist that the law is *neither in nor over* members of His church. Then what did the author of the epistle to the Hebrews mean? Are we to believe that *lawlessness* is in our hearts?

For further study: Ezek. 11:19; Matt. 5:17-20; 7:15-27; 15:1-9; 23:23; Rom. 8:4.

Question 37

How Can We Stop "Serving Sin" if We Disobey God's Law?

Knowing this, that our old man is crucified with him, that the body of sin might be destroyed, that henceforth we should not serve sin. For he that is dead is freed from sin (Romans 6:6-7).

The "old man" is the unregenerate person's *ethical* position as a spiritual heir to our father, Adam (Romans 5:12). It is this status which is removed from us when we are saved by grace. It is salvation which frees us from sin. Paul tells us to put off **"the old man, which is corrupt according to the deceitful lusts; and be renewed in the spirit of your mind; and that ye put on the new man, which after God is created in righteousness and true holiness"** (Ephesians 4:22-24). Again, the regenerate person has **"put on the new man, which is renewed in knowledge after the image of him that created him"** (Colossians 3:10).

What did Paul mean, **"renewed in knowledge"**? Did he mean that we have *less* knowledge than the saints in the Old Testament had concerning righteous behavior? Not at all. We have *better knowledge* than they had: this is the whole message of the epistle to the Ephesians (chapter 3 especially). We have *better revelation*. How can anyone seriously argue that with *greater knowledge* comes *reduced responsibility*? How can anyone seriously argue that with the coming of the New Testament, regenerate people need to pay *less* attention to God's law and its many applications in our lives? We are *dead to sin*. Why should we fear the law?

Questionable Answer

"Being freed from sin means being freed from the specific details of Old Testament law. We are adults now; we don't have God watching over our shoulders in order to punish us for every infraction of His law. We can now obey the Spirit."

My Reply: Does the Holy Spirit tell us to do things that were forbidden by Old Testament law? If so, then was the law imperfect? Rather, shouldn't we argue that the Holy Spirit tells us to obey the law in its entirety, unless a specific application of the law has been altered *by specific revelation in the New Testament*? If the New Testament hasn't specifically told us of a different application—for example, faith in Christ's *past* death and resurrection (the Book of Hebrews) rather than faith in slaughtered animals as a testimony of our faith in the *coming* sacrifice of the Messiah (Isaiah 53)—how can we trust our hearts to guide us if we do not have the law as a guideline? If our hearts are not *law-disciplined* and our actions are not therefore law-disciplined, how do we know when we are pleasing God? By "good feelings" concerning our actions? Then how are we different from the modern pagans, who say, "If it feels good, do it"?

Mature, responsible, self-disciplined adults don't abandon the righteous teachings of their parents when they leave the home of their parents. Rather, *they apply what they have learned*. They *keep* the laws their parents gave them as children, but they keep them as adults, not as children.

For further study: Deut. 10:12-13; Ps. 119:1-16; Ezek. 18:1-32; Mic. 6:8.

Question 38

Since God's Law Can't Kill Us, Won't It Help Us to Live?

> Now if we be dead with Christ, we believe that we shall also live with him: knowing that Christ being raised from the dead dieth no more; death hath no more dominion over him (Romans 6:8-9).

Christ did not need to die, for His life was sinless. Nevertheless, He did die, so that we will not die as a result of our sinful lives. When we speak of death, we mean the second death (Revelation 20:14). We still die physically, which points backward to our sinful origins, and points to our continuing ethical rebellions as intermittent violators of God's law.

We shall live with Him, meaning in the world beyond the grave. He was raised from physical death; so shall we also be raised from physical death (I Corinthians 15). Sin results in death—physical death, and then the second death of eternal punishment. Since sin in principle no longer reigns over us, neither does the second death. Thus, Paul wrote (not concerning physical death, but the second death): **"O death, where is thy sting? O grave, where is thy victory?"** (I Corinthians 15:55).

If death no longer reigns over us in principle, then *the threat of punishment* for our transgression of the law no longer reigns over us in principle. The threat of earthly punishment, yes. God still chastises us for our sins (Hebrews 12:5-7). The threat of physical death, yes. The consequence of Adam's transgression is with us still. But not the second death.

Questionable Answer

"Since we are dead in Christ, we cannot die the second death. Thus, we are no longer obliged to respect Old Testament law. Christ has paid the price. We live as free men—free from the burden of the law!"

My Reply: Yes, Christ paid the price. The death sentence which *sin* placed over us—a death sentence *manifested* by the law (but not created by it)—is removed. Our Father in Heaven has punished Christ rather than us. We are adopted ethically back into the regenerate family of God. No longer are we disinherited sons. But should adopted sons turn around and transgress the very laws that manifested their condition as disinherited sons?

We are still to respect Old Testament law, even though we don't fear its post-resurrection consequences. For one thing, *we know its **pre**-resurrection consequences*. There are earthly *blessings* associated with obedience to the law, and earthly *curses* associated with its transgression (Deuteronomy 28). But far more important, God wrote those laws, and the Father judged His Son for our transgression of them.

Throughout First John, we read that our ability to *test* our salvation—though not the foundation of our salvation—is based on the existence of Christ's commandments. Paul's words aren't opposed to John's. Paul respected the law as *a guideline for personal performance*, as John did. Do you? If not, why not?

For further study: I John 1:6-7; 2:3-6; 3:4, 10, 22-24; 5:2-3.

Question 39
How Can Sin Still "Reign" in Us if We Obey God's Law?

> **Likewise reckon ye also yourselves to be dead indeed unto sin, but alive unto God through Jesus Christ our Lord. Let not sin therefore reign in your mortal body, that ye should obey it in the lusts thereof** (Romans 6:11-12).

Paul warned us against letting sin reign in our mortal bodies. Obviously, sin cannot reign over our spiritual nature, which is redeemed, and which will go to be with God at our deaths. This nature will be reunited after the resurrection to perfect, corruption-free bodies (I Corinthians 15:42-44). But our *mortal bodies* still are subject to sinfulness. Never forget, **"the spirit indeed is willing, but the flesh is weak"** (Matthew 26:41).

How do we know when we are faced with a sinful temptation? How can we distinguish a temptation from an opportunity? Once again, we are back to that age-old question: *By what standard?* Paul tells us that our mortal bodies are still under the reign of sin. He warns us against this threat. The "lusts thereof" are with us still. In other words, *if we are no longer under the reign of sin in principle, because of Christ's death and resurrection, why should we allow ourselves to be ruled by sin in the flesh?*

The answer is clear: we must not allow our mortal bodies to be ruled by sin. We must discipline ourselves to avoid sin. But what is our criterion of sinful behavior, if not God's law? Humanism's standards?

Questionable Answer

"The way we escape from the rule of sin over our mortal bodies is to rely on the Spirit of God to lead us in the paths of righteousness. We are not to return to the details of Old Testament law."

My Reply: We are again faced with the task of *testing the spirits* to see if they are of God. If what we believe to be the Spirit of God tells us to do something contrary to the revealed, written word of God, why should we believe that the spirit informing our consciences is really God's Spirit? Satanists hear from spirits, too. Ethical rebels do what is right in their own eyes, but abominable in the sight of God. But how do we know what is abominable in the sight of God? And if we cannot be sure how we know, have we not returned to *ethical relativism*, the curse of modern humanist culture? What will distinguish our acts from the acts of the anti-God rebels? Does God's Spirit reign in us?

How can we rely on some sort of intuition to guide us, when intuition is notoriously unreliable, *unless it is informed by a detailed knowledge of God's comprehensive law*? How can we trust our consciences, *unless they are informed by a detailed knowledge of God's comprehensive law*? People are expelled from schools for reading evil material. What is "evil material," *Playboy* magazine, or this book? (We know which one causes more trouble for school administrators! Hint: it has no pictures.) How can we make righteous judgments about right and wrong if we reject God's standards of righteousness?

For further study: Ex. 20; Deut. 11:1-32; 28:15-68; Ps. 119:17-32.

Question 40
Aren't Those Who Disobey God's Law "Instruments of Unrighteousness"?

> **Neither yield ye your members as instruments of unrighteousness unto sin: but yield yourselves unto God, as those that are alive from the dead, and your members as instruments of righteousness unto God** (Romans 6:13).

We are to yield ourselves unto God, **"as those that are alive from the dead."** Why? Because we *are* alive from the dead! We are *ethically alive* and freed from the terror of the second death. But if we are ethically alive, then we should not act as those who are ethically dead. To "yield oneself unto God" is the same as *acting in conformity to God's law*. We are to be *imitators of Christ's perfect humanity*. He followed the law of God; so should we.

If this isn't true, then what can be meant by the phrase, "instruments of unrighteousness"? Doesn't this mean unregenerate bodies and minds? Isn't Paul contrasting these sin-governed instruments with instruments of righteousness? Should Christians walk in the same paths of unrighteousness as sinners do? When he says "members," doesn't Paul mean our thoughts and actions, since they reflect the state of each person's soul? In short, shouldn't *good fruit* be produced by *good plants*?

If sin no longer reigns over our immortal souls in the second death, why should sin reign over our members, meaning our mortal bodies? Isn't this what Paul keeps asking in Romans 6? Don't we need God's law to tell us if we meet God's test?

Questionable Answer

"We yield ourselves unto God when we love Him, and when we love His people. We pray to Him and respond to His answers to our prayers. This has nothing to do with Old Testament law."

My Reply: Paul made it clear in Romans 13:10 that love means the fulfillment of the law's precepts. **"Love worketh no ill to his neighbour: therefore love is the fulfilling of the law."** But how do we establish the details of what does or does not work ill to our neighbor, if not by God's law? What other standard is as reliable as God's revealed word? If we depart from the specific details of God's Old Testament law, unless we have explicit testimony to each and every alteration by a New Testament author, what will we substitute in its place? *By what standard?*

Our mortal bodies are to reveal our spiritual condition before God. If we are regenerate, shouldn't our visible actions, as well as our thoughts, conform to His eternal standards of righteousness (Matthew 5:28)? If we are immune from the second death, shouldn't our mortal bodies testify to others of God's grace to us in granting us this immunity? Shouldn't our actions point to life beyond the grave, rather than death beyond the grave? Shouldn't there be some sort of *ethical continuity* between our lives now and our lives beyond the grave? Shouldn't we grow in maturity as we grow older? Should we become lawless? How does Paul define lawlessness?

For further study: Ex. 21; Deut. 6:1-9, 16-25; 29:1-29; Ps. 119:33-56.

Question 41
What Does "Under Grace, Not Law" Mean?

For sin shall not have dominion over you: for ye are not under the law, but under grace (Romans 6:14).

Should we attempt to deal with this verse without surveying the verses that preceded it in chapter 6 of Romans? Obviously not. Yet there are many, many Bible teachers who try to do just this. They read into Paul's words what they would *like* for him to have said. But Paul was a logical man. He built up his arguments, step by step. What precedes a conclusion by Paul is crucial for understanding one of his conclusions.

Sin does not have dominion over our souls. This is a statement of fact, a description of our very nature as redeemed people. Paul argues this way throughout the passage (6:2, 4, 6-7). But sin *can* reign over our mortal bodies; it is still a threat to our witness (6:6, 11-13). He says **"henceforth we should not serve sin"** (6:6b). Got that? *Should* not. This is an *ethical command*, not a description of our redeemed nature. It is an "ought," not an "is."

How can Paul say that we are not under law, if he wants us to honor the law in our daily walk with God? Because he wants us to know that we are not under the *condemnation* of the law. We are not under the *curse* which confronts covenant-breakers. We are not to *fear* the law of God, for it no longer sentences us to the second death, as it did before Christ redeemed us. Instead, we are under grace, to do good works (Ephesians 2:8-10).

Questionable Answer

"A person cannot be under the law and not under the law at the same time. It's one or the other. God contrasts grace and law here. We are under grace and not under law. The law is a dead letter for us."

My Reply: It is not that the law is a dead letter to us. Rather, *we are a dead letter to the law*. We have *died ethically* as covenant-breakers, so that we may *live ethically* as covenant-keepers. The law no longer condemns us as regenerate men, who have the *perfect* righteousness of Christ imputed to them. But our *justification* (God's judicial decree of "not guilty") is not the same as our *progressive sanctification*, as we run the race, fight the good fight, and press on toward the mark for the prize of the high calling of God (Philippians 3:14). We receive justification at the time of our salvation, but this does not excuse us from working out our salvation with fear and trembling (Philippians 2:12b) — not in fear of losing our justification, but in fear of not attaining all that God would have us to achieve. (Warning: beware of contrasting God's predestination with our own personal responsibility, with respect either to justification or progressive sanctification. Paul says such logic is evil: Romans 9:20-23.) We honor the law *because* it cannot kill us.

If children grow too old to spank, should they become more rebellious, or should they have matured, showing greater respect? If we, as mature Christians, are free from the *penalty* of the law, shouldn't we be willing to obey it, in thankfulness?

For further study: Ex. 22; Lev. 18; Deut. 7:9-13; Ps. 119:57-80.

Question 42

Are We Free to Ignore God's Law if We Are "Under Grace"?

> What then? Shall we sin, because we are not under the law, but under grace? God forbid. Know ye not, that to whom ye yield yourselves servants to obey, his servants ye are to whom ye obey; whether of sin unto death, or of obedience unto righteousness? (Romans 6:15-16).

Can a man serve two masters? Can a man serve both God and Mammon? No (Matthew 6:24). Can a man wear Christ's yoke and Satan's? No (Matthew 11:29-30). Paul here has only followed Christ's teachings on the two kingdoms, Christ's and Satan's. Each has its own law-order, courts and sanctions, and promises. You choose to serve one or the other.

How do you know which person you serve? By your obedience. But obedience to what? Laws. Rules and regulations. We sing "onward, Christian soldiers," but do we really believe in this army? Have you ever seen an army without a book to "do it by"? Without a chain of command? Without a Commanding Officer?

Paul is offering us a warning here. *Determine who you serve by seeing whose laws you obey*. This is the very same warning we are given in First John. Yet there are Bible teachers who ignore this warning. They talk as if redeemed people can serve Christ without obeying the law of God—not as a means of *justification*, but as a means of *progressive sanctification*, both granted by God's grace.

Questionable Answer

"To tell people that they are under grace, not law, is not to tell them to sin. It is to state a biblical truth. You can't be under grace and still be under law. They are radically separate conditions."

My Reply: You cannot be under law as your means of justification. God won't declare you "not guilty" in His court of law on the basis of your works. To be under law as the basis of your justification is to perish in your sins. But what about your *progressive sanctification?* What about your walk with God? Don't you hope and pray that this ethical walk will improve over time? But if you hope and pray for this, *how will you determine whether your hopeful prayer has been answered?*

This is not a trick question. If you base your test of your walk with God on your feelings, then you are leaning on a weak reed. Bodily chemistry or shifts in your ability to enjoy your life are not God's criteria. There are people who are going to hell who say (and apparently do) feel terrific. Goliath sure seemed to have a progressive, confident, "power of positive thinking" sort of attitude. So did Jezebel.

Isn't the test of your walk with God the *law-revealed* fruit of your faith? "**What fruit had ye then in those things whereof ye are now ashamed? For the end of those things is death. . . . For the wages of sin is death**" (Romans 6:21, 23a).

If you want God's fruit, you must seek to obey God's law. This is New Testament doctrine.

For further study: Ps. 50:16; Matt. 7:21-23; Luke 6:46; II Tim. 2:19; Jas. 1:22.

Question 43

Is a Christian's "New Spirit" Opposed to God's Law?

> **For when we were in the flesh, the motions of sins [sinful passions—NASB], which were by the law, did work in our members to bring forth fruit unto death. But now we are delivered from the law, that being dead wherein we were held; that we should serve in newness of spirit, and not in the oldness of the letter** (Romans 7:5-6).

If we rely on our own works for our salvation, God's law only points out our sin and increases our guilt. It kills us. It binds us, as with a chain. Nevertheless, chains are useful tools. After all, Satan is bound with some sort of spiritual chain (Revelation 20:1)—or will be, say some Bible teachers. A chain can be used to bind evil men as prisoners or to lower an anchor and prevent a ship from drifting away.

In what way are we delivered from the law? As a supposed basis of our salvation (justification). The law no longer brings forth the second death in us. It no longer *binds* us. We serve God now in the "**newness of spirit, not in the oldness of the letter.**" But notice carefully: the contrast is *not* between "the letter of the law" and "the spirit of the law." It's between the *newness* of spirit and the *old* letter of the law. Does Paul say there is no such thing as the newness *for us* of the letter of God's law, when informed by God's Spirit? Of course not. This is what he teaches: *we* are made new, not God's standards.

Questionable Answer

"When we follow God's Spirit, we don't need to honor the details—the letter—of Old Testament law. It's our 'right attitude,' not the specific details of the law, that God honors."

My Reply: Weren't Old Testament people also supposed to have the "right attitude," both toward God and man? "**He hath shewed thee, O man, what is good; and what doth the LORD require of thee, but to do justly, and to love mercy, and to walk humbly with thy God?** (Micah 6:8). Many misinterpreted this requirement, which is why Micah and the prophets had to come and remind them about God's ethical demands on them. What was the message of the prophets? God wants *both*: sacrifices *and* a right attitude, but a right attitude was more important than the details of the rituals. (The best example of this is Hezekiah's prayer for the unclean people who wanted to celebrate Passover; God answered this prayer, and pardoned them [II Chronicles 29:17-21]).

Paul says that "**we should serve in newness of spirit.**" The question is: How do we know when we are serving obediently? The answer is obvious: the law of God tells us what we must do. But when we obey the specific terms of the law, our *attitude* should be one of joy, not sorrow. We serve as *free men*, redeemed by Christ's shed blood, not as bondmen, trapped by the killing power of God's law. The letter of the law should bring us joy.

For further study: Ex. 23:1-13; Lev. 19; Deut. 30:1-20; Ps. 119:81-104.

Question 44

Is the Law of God "Carnal" or Holy, Just, and Good?

For we know that the law is spiritual: but I am carnal, sold under sin (Romans 7:14).

Paul has led his readers through a complex argument. He has said that the very existence of the law of God was what made sin's presence known to him, and to all mankind. It was designed originally to give mankind a fuller, more productive life, but Adam and Eve misused God's commandment. **"And the commandment, which was ordained to life, I found to be unto death"** (v. 10). That was not God's fault; that was Paul's fault. His sin destroyed him. **"For sin, taking occasion by the commandment, deceived me, and by it slew me"** (v. 11). Paul's conclusion is unmistakably clear: **"Wherefore the law is holy, and just, and good"** (v. 12).

The law is not to be equated with sin; rather, it is to be *contrasted* with sin. **"What shall we say then? Is the law sin? God forbid. Nay, I had not known sin, but by the law: for I had not known lust, except the law had said, Thou shalt not covet"** (Romans 7:7). It was not the law which was Paul's enemy, but *sin*. **"Was then that which is good made death unto me? God forbid. But sin, that it might appear sin, working death in me by that which is good; that sin by the commandment might become exceeding sinful"** (v. 13).

Question: Why do so many Bible-believing Christians today not respect God's law as our *tool for identifying sin*?

Questionable Answer

"God's law was spiritual for the period of the Old Testament, but to regard it as ethically binding on Christians in the New Testament era is to make it carnal. Men are given the spirit of life today, not the spirit of bondage."

My Reply: Did faithful saints in the Old Testament experience release from the ethical bondage of sin? Yes. Did they still place themselves under Old Testament law as a moral guide? Paul said that he did, but the law slew him. Why? Because he was not yet regenerate. Even in his regenerate state, he saw the war between his redeemed spirit and his sinful lusts, called "the flesh." There were *two laws* warring in him: the *law of God* and the *law of sin*. **"But I see another law in my members, warring against the law of my mind, and bringing me into captivity to the law of sin which is in my members"** (v. 23). He cried out, **"Who shall deliver me from the body of this death?"** (v. 24). Then he answered his own question—an answer which contrasts the two laws in his life: **"I thank God through Jesus Christ our Lord. So then with the mind I myself serve the law of God; but with the flesh, the law of sin"** (v. 25).

Are there two different laws? *Subjectively*, yes. *Objectively*, no. Paul's "old man" was still being killed by the sentence of God's law. But his renewed mind was given life by that same law code.

If we wish to subdue the "old man" in our lives, we must use God's law to do so, just as Paul did. There is no other way.

For further study: Ps. 119:21; Rom. 3:20; 4:15; 5:13; I John 3:14.

Question 45
How Can We "Walk after the Spirit" if We Disobey God's Law?

There is therefore now no condemnation to them which are in Christ Jesus, who walk not after the flesh, but after the Spirit. For the law of the Spirit of life in Christ Jesus hath made me free from the law of sin and death" (Romans 8:1-2).

Paul has argued that the law was sin's instrument in killing him. But here he says that the law was also the Spirit's instrument of putting him back on God's holy path. When he was an ethical rebel, the law gave occasion to his enemy, sin, to slay him. But once he was converted by grace, that same law gave him light to illuminate the path of righteousness. Had the law changed? Paul never said so. On the contrary, he shows how *he had changed*, not God's law. God changes sinners, not His law.

Paul argues that the flesh is so weak that *the law did not make the contrast plain enough*, so that he did not fully understand the contrast between sin and righteousness, between spiritual death and spiritual life. It took the advent of Christ to make clear the radical contrast between sinful flesh and perfect flesh. (Warning: not perfect divinity, but perfect flesh —perfect *humanity*.) **"For what the law could not do, in that it was weak through the flesh, God sending his own Son in the likeness of sinful flesh, and for sin, condemned sin in the flesh: That the righteousness of the law might be fulfilled in us, who walk not after the flesh, but after the Spirit"** (vv. 3-4).

Questionable Answer

"The contrast Paul speaks about is between 'law' and 'grace.' It is not some hypothetical contrast between the response of fallen man to God's law and the response of redeemed man to that same law. The law curses us, and the Spirit gives us life. We should follow God's Spirit, not God's law."

My Reply: If the contrast is between the specifics of God's law and an anti-biblical law (antinomian) position, why does Paul repeatedly tell us that the law is holy and good? Why would God set aside a holy and good thing? Because God's law allows sin to kill sinful man? But Paul rejoiced in the death of the old man, the old Adam who adopts the ethics of rebellion. What a wonderful evangelical tool God's law is: it progressively kills this old Adam.

Law does more than serve as the slayer of the old Adam. Coupled with the gospel of salvation, *it empowers men to live righteously*. The same law that points to the second death at the end of a man's lifetime, and warns him to get off the broad path that leads to destruction, also points out the narrow way that leads to the judgment of God. In principle, God has already pronounced judgment on His people: "Not guilty!" This is the meaning of *justification*. But before He *publicly* pronounces this same judgment on the day of final judgment, we must walk in the path of righteousness prescibed by the law: *progressive sanctification*. God first *declares* us righteous (justification); then we work out the implications of our faith by means of God's law.

For further study: Lev. 20:8; Deut. 6:25; 24:13; Ps. 119:105-128.

Question 46

Isn't a "Carnal Mind" One Which Is Opposed to God's Law?

For to be carnally minded is death; but to be spiritually minded is life and peace. Because the carnal mind is enmity against God: for it is not subject to the law of God, neither indeed can be. So then they that are in the flesh cannot please God (Romans 8:6-8).

We are confronted by the *same contrast* which marks the preceding verses: the carnal or fleshly mind vs. the spiritual mind. The carnal mind is in opposition to God and His will. It cannot obey God's law, so those who are unregenerate cannot please God. This is a variation of Paul's contrast between the natural man and the spiritual man. The natural man will not receive the teachings of the Spirit (I Corinthians 2:14).

What is the characteristic feature of the carnal mind? It refuses to be subject to God's law. Unregenerate people do the deeds of the flesh, but they who are spiritual do the deeds of the Spirit (Romans 8:5). What are the deeds of the flesh? They are actions that violate the law of God. This is what Paul said condemned him before God. **"For the good that I would [should do] I do not; but the evil which I would not [should not do], that I do"** (Romans 7:19).

To what did Paul contrast this condition? Obeying the law of God: **"For I delight in the law of God after the inward man"** (7:22). This is the law of God written on the heart of the regenerate person (Hebrews 8:7-10).

Questionable Answer

"Those who are regenerate do righteous actions naturally, for their natures are changed. They do not need to study Old Testament law to tell them what they should do. They know instinctively. The Spirit of God leads them through life, step by step."

My Reply: Will the Spirit of God lead redeemed men to do things in opposition to God's revealed law? Isn't one of the tests that we are supposed to apply to our own decision-making the revelation of God concerning His law? How do we know where we got the idea to do this or that? Did the idea originate in our carnal minds, which are still at war with our spiritual minds, as they were in Paul? Or from some demonic source? Or from God Himself? *We test our thoughts by means of God's law.*

Paul says elsewhere: **"Study to show thyself approved unto God, a workman that needeth not to be ashamed, rightly dividing the word of truth"** (II Timothy 2:15). Why study, if we have the law written in our hearts? Because what is written *definitively* in our hearts—imparted at the time of our regeneration through definitive sanctification (Christ's righteousness applied to us)—is not *applied* to our lives until we study the revealed law and begin working out its implications. We know God, too, but that doesn't mean we are to stop studying the Bible in search of a better understanding. We are to study even more!

Christians possess new natures *in principle*. These natures must be worked out *in history*. God's law helps us work out our new natures in history.

For further study: Lev. 20; 26; Ps. 119:129-152.

Question 47

How Can We "Mortify the Flesh" if We Disobey God's Law?

> For if ye live after the flesh, ye shall die: but if ye through the Spirit do mortify the deeds of the body, ye shall live. For as many as are led by the Spirit of God, they are the sons of God (Romans 8:13-14).

Paul contrasts *two different minds:* carnal and spiritual. When we read "flesh," we must interpret it accordingly. This doesn't mean that Paul was some sort of materialistic determinist. He didn't mean that our decisions are a function of our chemistry, or that our bodies control our minds. He meant that there are *two warring principles of interpretation*: the flesh and the spirit. This same contrast was present in the Garden of Eden.

When a person is unregenerate, his attempts to live consistently according to God's law must fail. The war of his carnal mind against the law of God delivers him into death. Sin captures him, Paul said. *But a regenerate man progressively conquers the lusts of the flesh.* How? Through the empowering of the Holy Spirit—the Spirit's action in helping him to apply the principles of biblical law to every area of life.

What Paul describes is a *war*. Wars involve conflict. *Wars also demand self-discipline in terms of a rule book*. The carnal mind has its rule book: defy God and His law. The spiritual mind has its rule book: honor God and His law. We follow **"the Spirit of truth"** who leads us into all truth (John 16:13). Does this Spirit call God's law (which He co-authored) a lie?

Questionable Answer

"We mortify the deeds of the body by avoiding evil acts. The Spirit tells us what is wrong, and then He gives us the power to avoid sin (I Corinthians 10:13). By taking heed of the details of Old Testament law, we become carnal again, submitting ourselves to the law that kills."

My Reply: What has Paul argued? Not that the law of God kills the regenerate, but that it allows sin to kill the *unrighteous*. The law of God he calls holy, just, and good (7:12). How can something written by God, declared to be perfect (Psalm 19:7), and described by Paul as holy, just, and good, be the pathway back to domination by the carnal mind? On the contrary, Paul describes it as a means of subduing the evil deeds of the flesh, but a means that can be used successfully only by regenerate people. God's law is our guideline that tells us the step-by-step program of Christian *self-government*: God's program of *progressive personal sanctification*.

Paul calls the Holy Spirit **"the Spirit of adoption"** (Romans 8:15). This is the biblical doctrine of *ethical adoption*. All men are sons of God in terms of God's creation (Acts 17:26)—*disinherited sons* as a result of Adam's sin. But Christians are adopted sons. **"The Spirit itself beareth witness with our spirit, that we are the children of God"** (Romans 8:16). How do we test this Spirit? God's law.

Yet there are Bible teachers who tell us that God's law no longer is a valid test of the spirits. Amazing!

For further study: Ps. 119:153-176; I Cor. 9:24-27; Col. 3:1-10; Titus 2:11-12.

Question 48
Didn't Paul Believe That the Specifics of God's Law Still Apply?

For the scripture saith, Thou shalt not muzzle the ox that treadeth out the corn. And, The labourer is worthy of his reward (I Timothy 5:18).

Deuteronomy 25:4 governs the treatment of oxen that are used in the fields. It is one of the more obscure laws in the Old Testament. Nevertheless, Paul cited it in order to demonstrate the moral necessity of paying ministers and elders for their services (I Timothy 5:17). Something as important as financial support of the ministry of preaching and ruling was subsumed by Paul under this "obscure" Old Testament law.

This law is a *case-law application* of the general principle of equity or fairness in the Bible. It is a specific application of the principle, "Do unto others as you would have others do unto you." But Paul cited Deuteronomy, not Jesus' "golden rule."

The Old Testament law provides both the general principles, which we call the Ten Commandments, and the specific applications, which lawyers call case laws. The specifics of the law were never intended to be divorced from the general principles of equity or fairness. The "spirit" of the law is seen in the general principles of equity; the "letter" of the law is seen in specific examples. Both are required by God.

Why would Paul have cited as morally binding an "obscure" Old Testament law? Because that law was never intended to be obscure! It is obscure to us, not to God (and to the oxen).

Questionable Answer

"Paul used this obscure rule only as an example. He did not mean that it would always be immoral to keep oxen from eating corn in the fields. So it is with all of the Old Testament laws: they are only moral examples."

My Reply: Quite true: they are indeed moral examples. Question: Do we honor a moral example by violating its explicit terms? Do we honor this principle by muzzling oxen? Isn't the general principle more likely to become obscured to the minds of sinful men than the explicit examples? Don't the explicit examples keep our eyes fixed on the true meaning of the general principles of equity? *If we close our eyes to the **specific details** of the example, how will we be certain that we are honoring the general principle in other cases?* After all, this is precisely what Paul warned Timothy about: Christians who were unwilling to support the ministry of the church leaders.

We violate the *general principle* when we violate the *details*. A so-called "moral example" is valid morally precisely because it is *morally binding*. If it were not morally binding, how could it be a moral example? Are we to honor the spirit of the law while breaking the explicit example? Aren't the examples binding if the general principle is binding? And if the examples aren't binding, what will pull men back from evil interpretations?

Once again, we must ask that crucial question: *By what standard?*

For further study: Mark 10:3-7; Acts 23:1-5; I Cor. 9:9-10; 14:34; II Cor. 6:16-18; 13:1; Gal. 5:14; Eph. 6:1-3; Jas. 2:9-11.

Question 49

How Can We Separate the "Moral Law" from God's Laws?

Think not that I am come to destroy the law, or the prophets: I am not come to destroy, but to fulfil. For verily I say unto you, Till heaven and earth pass, one jot or one tittle shall in no wise pass from the law, till all be fulfilled. Whosoever therefore shall break one of these least commandments, and shall teach men so, he shall be called the least in the kingdom of heaven: but whosoever shall do and teach them, the same shall be called great in the kingdom of heaven (Matthew 5:17-19).

Jesus was very clear: *God's law is a unified whole*. The tiniest Hebrew letter, the "jot," or "yode," as we pronounce the Hebrew, is to be maintained, **"till heaven and earth pass."** The Old Covenant heavens and earth departed with the coming of the New Covenant. But Jesus went on to say that in the New Covenant **kingdom of heaven**, we are great only if we do **all** the commandments, down to the **least**. Christians are to take heed, in some sense, to all of the law.

The question is this: Are all Old Testament laws still binding in their details? Not if Christ's life, death, and resurrection have altered a law's *application*. But all Old Testament laws are *moral* laws. Jesus didn't distinguish "moral laws" from "ceremonial laws." We sometimes find specific New Testament teaching that a particular Old Testament law is to be *honored in a different way* in the New Testament era. But we may never *abandon* any Old Testament law in principle.

Questionable Answer

"Jesus fulfilled the requirements of all of God's Old Testament laws. We no longer have to honor them, for they are *fulfilled*. They have passed away. We need only honor the spirit of the moral law, not the details."

My Reply: The question is: How can we determine the "spirit" of the "moral law"? *Unless* we have specific New Testament instructions concerning required changes in application of a specific law, do we dare disobey any law of God? Since *all the law of God is a moral law,* we must not distinguish one law from another in terms of a false distinction: "moral law" vs. "ceremonial law."

Yes, Christ perfectly fulfilled the terms of the law. But He spoke not of the law passing away, but of heaven and earth passing away *before* the law passes away. So why should Christians believe that any Old Testament law has passed away ("died") because of Christ's earthly ministry? How can Christians legitimately believe that Christ's perfect life in any way abolished *any* of the laws of God? (Remember: an altered application *isn't* the same as abolition.) Didn't Jesus say specifically that anyone who teaches such a doctrine will be "**the least in the kingdom of heaven**"? Don't you take this warning seriously?

If you disagree, then you need to read Chapter 2 of Greg L. Bahnsen's book, *Theonomy in Christian Ethics*. Soon. Your instructor had better read it even sooner. Ask questions.

For further study: Josh. 22:5; Ps. 93:5; 111:7-8; 119:152, 160; Luke 16:17; II Tim. 3:16-17; Heb. 12:14; Jas. 2:10; Rev. 22:14.

Question 50

Doesn't Faith in Christ Establish God's Law?

Do we then make void the law through faith? God forbid: yea, we establish the law (Romans 3:31).

Paul could not have made his position any plainer. Nevertheless, there are millions of Bible-believing Christians who teach that Paul was hostile to Old Testament law as a moral guideline for ethical action. They teach that Paul stood against the law of God, recommending in its place a sort of mystical union with the Holy Spirit—a union which is not supposed to be tested by the believer in terms of the specifics of biblical law. They refuse to see that God's law tests *all* spirits!

What could Paul possibly have meant by the phrase, **"yea, we establish the law"**? Isn't this what Jesus said in Matthew 5:17-18—that He came not to annul the law but to fulfill (or establish) it? Why are modern expositors so hostile to the words of Paul and Jesus? Is it because they are unwilling to accept the light burden of Jesus' ethical yoke, and instead believe that they can carry a better yoke than Jesus'?

Faith does not make void or empty God's law. The grace of God enables a regenerate man to begin to use the law of God as a *tool of dominion*: first, in his own spiritual life; second, in his external relationships with others; and third, in the progressive construction of the kingdom of God, in time and on earth, and subsequently, beyond the grave, after the resurrection. The law is a *curse* to the sinner and a *blessing* to us.

Questionable Answer

"When Paul said that 'we establish the law,' he didn't mean for this age. He meant for the millennial kingdom, after Christians are given perfect bodies and no longer are subject to death, and when they will rule the whole earth—not yet transfigured or even converted to faith in Christ—with a rod of iron."

My Reply: Paul was writing to New Testament Christians living in Rome. If this was not "the church age," what is? He gave the church at Rome a lesson in biblical law. He told them specifically that *we* establish the law. Who did he mean? Obviously, "we" refers here to Christians living in Paul's day who were working out their salvations with fear and trembling (Philippians 2:12b). "We" does not refer to those people who supposedly will reign with Christ in perfected bodies after one resurrection but before another resurrection a thousand years later. "We" refers to those people who called themselves Christians and who were contemporaries of Christians living in Rome in Paul's day.

If we find ourselves preaching sermons (or listening to sermons without at least mental resistance) that attempt to "make void the law," then *we* are in rebellion morally, not Paul. We are denying the ethical requirement that we establish the law. We are at war with Jesus Christ. We will be disciplined. Therefore we must change our attitude toward God's law: **"For the time is come that judgment must begin at the house of God: and if it first begin at us, what shall the end be of them that obey not the gospel of God?"** (I Peter 4:17).

For further study: Lev. 22:31-33; Matt. 5:17-20; 23:23; Rom. 8:3-4.

Recommended Reading
(an asterisk marks outstanding works)

Adams, Jay E. *Competent to Counsel*. Nutley, NJ: Presbyterian and Reformed, 1970.

Bahnsen, Greg L. *By This Standard*. Tyler, TX: Institute for Christian Economics, 1985.

*_____. *Theonomy in Christian Ethics*. Nutley, NJ: Craig Press, (1977) 1984. This book will devastate your antinomian instructors. They cannot answer it.

Bolton, Samuel. *The True Bounds of Christian Freedom*. Reprint edition; London: Banner of Truth, 1964. (17th century)

Chantry, Walter. *Today's Gospel: Authentic or Synthetic?* Edinburgh: Banner of Truth, 1970.

*Jordan, James B. *The Law of the Covenant: An Exposition of Exodus 21-23*. Tyler, TX: Institute for Christian Economics, 1984.

Kaiser, Walter C. *Toward Old Testament Ethics*. Grand Rapids: Zondervan, 1983.

Kevan, Ernest F. *The Grace of Law: A Study of Puritan Theology*. Grand Rapids: Baker, (1963) 1983.

Lauxstermann, E. M. *The Believer's Delight*. Nutley, NJ: Presbyterian and Reformed, 1975.

Murray, John. *Principles of Conduct: Aspects of Biblical Ethics*. Grand Rapids: Eerdmans, 1957.

North, Gary. *Moses and Pharaoh*. Tyler, TX: Institute for Christian Economics, 1985.

_____. *The Sinai Strategy*. Tyler, TX: Institute for Christian Economics, 1986.

_____. *Tools of Dominion*. Tyler, TX: Institute for Christian Economics, 1990.

_____. *The Dominion Covenant: Genesis*. Tyler, TX: Institute for Christian Economics, 1982.

_____. *Unconditional Surrender: God's Program for Victory*. 3rd edition; Ft. Worth, TX: Dominion Press, 1988.

_____, ed. *The Journal of Christian Reconstruction*, Vol. II, No. 2: Symposium on Biblical Law. (This journal is published by the Chalcedon Foundation, P.O. Box 158, Vallecito, CA 95251.)

_____, ed. *The Journal of Christian Reconstruction*, Vol. V, No. 1: Symposium on Politics.

Rushdoony, Rousas John. *By What Standard?* Tyler, TX: Thoburn Press, (1959) 1983.

*_____. *The Institutes of Biblical Law*. Nutley, NJ: Craig Press, 1973. This book will show exactly how crucial biblical law is, and has been, in Western civilization.

_____. *Politics of Guilt and Pity*. Fairfax, VA: Thoburn Press, 1978.

Vos, J. G. *The Separated Life*. Philadelphia: Great Commission Publications, n.d.

Williamson, G. I. *Wine in the Bible and the Church*. Phillipsburg, NJ: Pilgrim Publishing Co., 1976.

Part III
KINGDOM: GOD'S OR MAN'S

Introduction to Part III

Jesus said, **"by their fruits ye shall know them"** (Matthew 7:20). If this rule applies to every person in his moral life, doesn't it also apply to societies? Wouldn't a society made up entirely of Christians who personally obey God's laws look a lot different from a society filled with humanists who reject God's law? The answer should be obvious. But apparently it isn't obvious, because there are a lot of Christian leaders who openly assert that there is no such thing as Bible-based standards for a New Testament era Christian society, Christian culture, or Christian anything (except a church). Only when Christ comes in person to reign on earth for a thousand years before the final judgment will we see a Bible-based society established. (They believe in a millennium, in other words.) But this period of peace and prosperity will be run as a theocratic bureaucracy—a centralized government with Jesus reigning personally as a total dictator. It will not be a world that comes as a result of the power of Christ's gospel, but only as a result of Christ's personal power as God ruling on earth. (In short, they don't believe in the power of the gospel by itself to transform societies.)

There are some Christian leaders (mainly people with a Dutch background) who argue that there are indeed biblical standards for every area of life, but that these standards will always be rejected by society. There will never be sufficient numbers of Christians to constitute a true Christian society, and therefore these standards will never be applied before Christ's second coming at the end of time. (They don't believe in the millennium, in other words.) The kingdom of humanist man will triumph.

Which position is correct? Neither.

What the Bible teaches is that God's kingdom, however imperfect, will be established on earth prior to the return of Christ. This kingdom will be visible institutionally. It will be empowered by grace, for large numbers of people will be converted to faith in Christ, though not everyone need be converted in order to have this visible kingdom established. It will be marked by the rule of God's law. It won't be a centralized, top-down authoritarian system over people who resist Christ's rule, for the bulk of the population will voluntarily submit to the rule of Christ's principles in every area of their lives.

This will happen *before* Christ returns physically to render final judgment. Remember, the wheat and the tares grow together in the field until the day of final judgment (Matthew 13:3-8, 18-30). So there *will* be a millennium of peace. There *will* be a rule of Christ's law on earth before the final judgment. There *are* explicitly biblical standards for a Christian society as well as for Christian individuals. In short, *there really is hope*. Our good work today *will* make a difference for Christ's Kingdom.

The humanists deny all this. They believe that the teachings of the Bible will become ever less important. Too many Christians agree with the humanists. They are therefore theologically and intellectually compromised. The Bible says that *the gospel will be victorious*, that it will eventually conquer all institutions. If you think I'm incorrect about this, read the next 25 questions.

Question 51

Aren't Those Who Obey God's Law the "Salt of the Earth"?

> **Ye are the salt of the earth: but if the salt have lost his savour, wherewith shall it be salted? It is thenceforth good for nothing, but to be cast out, and to be trodden underfoot of men** (Matthew 5:13).

Salt is used to make foods tastier. It is also a preservative, but Jesus was using the metaphor of flavor.

Salt is known all over the world as a valuable resource. It has even served as money in some cultures, since it is divisible, easily recognized, durable, transportable, and scarce (at least in primitive societies). But without its flavor, what good would it be? It would function only as an inhibitor to growth. This is why victorious armies in ancient civilization would spread salt over a defeated city: to "salt it over," so that nothing would grow there in the future (Judges 9:45).

Christians are to improve the world, in the same way that salt improves flavor in otherwise bland, tasteless foods. How are they to do this? With their *good works*, which is the focus of this passage (v. 16). Remove a Christian's good works, and he is no better than tasteless salt in the eyes of the world.

How are we to discern what good works are? We return to that now-familiar question: *By what standard?* And we come up with that now-familiar answer: *biblical law*. We use the revelation of God concerning His character and our standards of action to serve as the salt of the earth.

Questionable Answer

"It is true that our good works make us salt in the eyes of men. But to try to enforce biblical law over all men would be to make us worse than flavorless in the eyes of men. They would spit us out and throw us and our message away. Too much salt tastes terrible; it can even kill you."

My Reply: How much salt is too much? Our taste buds tell us. But tastes can change. So are we simply at the mercy of the anti-God, anti-law (antinomian) taste buds of the unbelieving world? Should they tell us how much biblical law they want? Are they the best judges of how much salt is good for them and the society?

The Bible gives us our standard. It tells us that we need to use God's law to determine what we should do *personally*. We are to respect it. But then why is it so unreliable in the other areas? Why is the law of God to be "salted over" by Christians who refuse to honor it? Why shouldn't God's law govern everyone?

We start with good works in our own lives. We gain the confidence of the anti-God world. But our goal is *comprehensive flavoring*. We are to flavor all the world's institutions with the flavor of God's law, in time and on earth. We increase men's fondness for the flavor of salt by conducting ourselves honorably. Then, as time goes on, we can extend God's kingdom by flavoring the whole civilization.

And if we refuse, are we not salt that has lost its savor?

For further study: Ps. 2:7-9; 22:27-31; 72; Matt. 28:19-20; Rev. 2:26-27.

Question 52

Isn't a "City on a Hill" to Be an Example for the World?

Ye are the light of the world. A city that is set on an hill cannot be hid. Neither do men light a candle, and put it under a bushel, but on a candlestick; and it giveth light unto all that are in the house (Matthew 5:14-15).

Christ's basic message to us in this passage is that we are to be examples of righteousness in the world. This light is to be individual, and it is also collective: in the church, and wherever Christians exercise authority in any institution.

The evangelical function of the "city on a hill" parallels the evangelical function of the whole Old Testament commonwealth.

> **Behold, I have taught you statutes and judgments, even as the LORD my God commanded me, that ye should do so in the land whither ye go to possess it. Keep therefore and do them; for this is your wisdom and your understanding in the sight of the nations, which shall hear all these statutes, and say, Surely this great nation is a wise and understanding people. For what nation is there so great, who hath God so nigh unto them, as the Lord our God is in all things that we call upon him for?** (Deuteronomy 4:5-7).

Biblical law is the very foundation of God's civilization.

Questionable Answer

"The 'city on a hill' may sound as though it represents an entire civilization, but it is only figurative for the way we run our churches. We are to be good examples as the body of Christ. But this passage has no application at all in society. We are not a city, as Israel was: separate from other cities. We are mixed into the society as a whole."

My Reply: The "nations" continue to exist separately right into the final days. Speaking of the heavenly city, which is the New Jerusalem, **"And the nations of them which are saved shall walk in the light of it: and the kings of the earth do bring their glory and honour into it"** (Revelation 21:24). As Christian cultures develop toward that day, aren't we serving as *lights to all nations* in every case where the gospel becomes a shaping influence in any one nation? Shouldn't we strive to create a society which will *shine ethically* before other nations, just as we try to do in our families, our churches, and our businesses?

Obviously, this passage applies to both individuals and groups of Christians. Yet many Bible teachers draw an arbitrary line at politics and say, "Thus far, and no farther, Jesus. Your word does not speak to this area of life. Yes, Israel was supposed to shine, and Israel had less light than we do, for you have come. But Christians have *less* responsibility!"

A godly society before pagans was an important aspect of evangelism in the Old Testament. Why not today?

For further study: Ps. 86:9; 87; Isa. 2:2-4; 60:1-9; Phil. 2:15; I Pet. 2:9-12.

Question 53
Should We Limit the Areas to Be Illuminated by Our "Light"?

Let your light so shine before men, that they may see your good works, and glorify your Father which is in heaven (Matthew 5:16).

Jesus' words here are also repeated in I Peter 2:12: **"Having your conversation honest among the Gentiles: that, whereas they speak against you as evildoers, they may by your good works, which they shall behold, glorify God in the day of visitation."**

The perspective of both Peter and Paul is that *the good works that regenerate men perform can make a difference culturally*. Men who see that God's word has positive effects in the ethical lives of others will be moved to glorify God, even if they are not converted. Unregenerate men, despite their position as covenant-breakers, nevertheless normally have enough knowledge of good and evil that they prefer to have good done unto them by their neighbors.

The gospel has beneficial effects outside the immediate community of believers. Why? *Because the gospel deals with ethical life in the real world*. Question: Should Christians argue that these good effects are limited exclusively to family and church? How about neighborhood? How about education? How about business dealings? But if the gospel has positive effects in these areas of personal responsibility, what about others? What about politics, law, and management? How can we legitimately exclude *any* area of light-shining?

Questionable Answer

"Christians are responsible before God for the conduct of their personal lives. They are not responsible for the institutions of this world, which are exclusively Satan's property. It is futile to attempt social reform by good example. Satan owns this world."

My Reply: Why then should we let our lights shine? Merely as testimonies to bring rebellious people to saving faith? If this testimony is successful, and many former pagans accept the lordship of Christ in their lives, what then? Are we obliged to tell them to abdicate their present positions of authority? Are we supposed to tell them that they are no longer responsible for the proper exercise of such authority, now that they are no longer Satan's servants? Are they supposed to quit their jobs? Or are we to tell them to search the word of God for ethical and *institutional guidelines* for the godly exercise of authority?

Does the gospel's light not throw light on every area of life? Are we therefore not responsible as individuals before God to exercise dominion over our personal zones of responsible decision-making? But how shall we exercise such responsibility? Using what rules? *By what standard?*

God's revealed law gives us guidance in the areas of economics, civil government, history, and education. Why should we ignore His law when we find ourselves in responsible positions? Why not do our best to get His laws enforced?

For further study: Deut. 10:14; Ps. 24:1; Matt. 28:18; Eph. 1:20-22; Phil. 2:9-10.

Question 54
How Can Christians Be Resurrected before the Millennium?

> He said unto them, An enemy hath done this. The servants said unto him, Wilt thou then that we go and gather them up? But he said, Nay; lest while ye gather up the tares, ye root up also the wheat with them. Let both grow together until the harvest: and in the time of harvest I will say to the reapers, Gather ye together first the tares, and bind them in bundles to burn them: but gather the wheat into my barn (Matthew 13:28-30).

Jesus' parable of the wheat and the tares shows us what we can expect in history. Jesus explained that the devil sowed the tares in the field, which is the world. The harvest is the end of the world. The reapers are the angels (13:38-39). Thus, *there is no break in history—no gathering of believers to God—before the end of the world*. There will be no "secret rapture" which takes place at the beginning of the millennium, or seven years before the millennium. There is no *discontinuous event* between now and the second coming of Christ in final judgment. The tares, meaning evil people, are gathered out of the field (the world) first, not the Christians.

There is growth unto destruction (tares) and growth unto final victory (wheat). There is maturity in both ethical camps. Neither side is cut out ("cuts out") of history before the end of time. There is *continuity* between our works now and a millennial age.

Questionable Answer

"We are not to understand this parable as a complete description of history. It only points out that there is good and evil until the day of judgment."

My Reply: What is noticeable in the parable is how forcefully the owner of the field resists the idea of removing the tares from the wheat. The idea is to get the tares out of the field, said his servants. No, the husbandman corrected them, we must protect the wheat. If you try to uproot the tares prematurely, you will uproot some wheat. *Let both tares and wheat develop to full maturity*, and then the reapers (angels) can harvest the tares first and burn them, leaving the wheat intact.

What is not even considered in the parable is the idea that the wheat should be removed from the field, leaving the *tares* to grow without competition! The servants were not so foolish as to suggest that the tares should receive the benefits of being cared for in the field, while the opportunity to mature is removed from the now-uprooted wheat. Yet it is this latter vision which has been preached by many Bible teachers. They teach that Christians will be removed miraculously from the "field" (the world), while the tares go on growing. In short, the salt will be removed—the city on a hill, the light that shines before men. The ethical testimony of the church will be gone. Jesus' parable absolutely denies such teachings!

Since Jesus taught this, why do Christians refuse to believe it?

For further study: Dan. 12:2; Matt. 25:31-32; John 5:27-29; 6:39-40, 44, 54; 11:24; Acts 24:15; Rev. 20:13.

Question 55
Doesn't God's Kingdom Grow Slowly Until It Fills the Earth?

> **Another parable put he forth unto them, saying, The kingdom of heaven is like to a grain of mustard seed, which a man took, and sowed in his field: which indeed is the least of all seeds: but when it is grown, it is the greatest among herbs, and becometh a tree, so that the birds of the air come and lodge in the branches thereof** (Matthew 13:31-32).

What was Jesus' point? Simple: as we build the kingdom of God, in time and on earth, we shouldn't expect major miraculous leaps. We should expect a *process of maturation*. As we grow in faith and competence, we will see more and more of Christ's influence in the world. Jesus was telling the disciples that they shouldn't expect some major cataclysmic event to turn them into a massive army overnight. No, the kingdom is like a tiny mustard seed which grows to become an influence later on. Starting small, the church will experience success over time.

The process of biological growth is marked by *continuity*. It is slow. It is relatively steady. It is not uniform throughout all periods, of course. Some periods are marked by greater or lesser speed in development. But the disciples were warned against expecting overnight success.

At the same time, they were warned not to expect any permanent setback. The mustard seed eventually grows to such a size that it provides a resting place for the birds. It perseveres.

Questionable Answer

"The mustard seed is a hearty plant. It does grow from small beginnings. But it is no oak. It is not like grass. It neither covers the earth nor reaches to the sky. It is successful only in comparison to its small origin."

My Reply: The whole thrust of this parable is that the *comparative growth* of the mustard plant is spectacular. It starts so incredibly small, and it grows proportionately to a huge size. Christ was not comparing a mustard tree to oaks; He was comparing it to its tiny seed. He was calling attention to the tremendous disparity between the seed and the mature adult tree.

This is what the kingdom of God is like. It started very small—a tiny sect in a tiny nation in the midst of a massive empire. Yet as time has gone on, the church and the church's influence have grown. (The kingdom is not equated by Christ to the church; the church is one aspect of the kingdom.) The influence of Christians in many fields has increased. This influence has not been uniform in every century. Some centuries have been eras of cultural retreat for Christians. (Our own era is just such a period.) Nevertheless, the mustard tree is not uprooted. God keeps it in the ground, growing in influence, and eventually providing a resting place for others. The kingdom of God will grow as a plant does, until final maturity.

There is no period of "uprooted mustard tree" in which only evil-doers remain on earth to mature in their sin. There is *continuity of development*, both for good and evil.

For further study: Jer. 31:31-34; Ezek. 47:1-12; Mic. 4:1-4; Hab. 2:14; Hag. 2:7-9.

Question 56
Doesn't "Leaven" Mean Victory?

Another parable spake he unto them; The kingdom of heaven is like unto leaven, which a woman took, and hid in three measures of meal, till the whole was leavened" (Matthew 13:33).

First of all, let's get one thing perfectly clear: "Leaven" *doesn't* mean "sin." Leavened bread was required by God for an important Old Testament sacrifice, the peace offering of thanksgiving (Leviticus 7:13). Unleavened bread was required at the Passover, as a symbol of the separation of Israel from the corrupt ethical leaven of Egypt. But once in the promised land, they were *required* to bring *leavened* bread before God. At the feast of Pentecost, they were required to bake leaven loaves as the firstfruits offering (Leviticus 23:17). This was the leaven of *ethical maturity*, the best bread of the land. If we were to equate "leaven" with "evil," we would call into question the decision of God in requiring a symbol of evil in a thanksgiving sacrifice to Him. *The leavened offering was characteristic of Pentecost, a day of rejoicing*.

What is leaven? It is *yeast*. A little is put into dough before it is baked. It causes the dough to rise. It produces a soft, full loaf. Leaven is a symbol of *growth*, of maturity or development. It can refer either to evil or righteousness. We are to put away the old leaven, the corrupt leaven (I Corinthians 5:6-8). But the kingdom is like leaven: *growth is basic*.

Questionable Answer

"Yes, the kingdom grows. It grows spiritually. Those who are part of the church do mature spiritually over time. But this says nothing about the influence of the kingdom in history. It does not replace Satan's corrupt leaven loaf."

My Reply: Unquestionably, the premise of the growth of God's kingdom is *the ethical maturing of His people over time*. But this is not simply growth within one person's lifetime. It is *growth throughout history* This parable is like the parables that preceded it. *Its setting is **world history***.

What is growing is a specifically Christian civilization. The parables do not describe just one individual's spiritual development. The focus is on a collective entity, the kingdom. This kingdom is made up of all Christians. It isn't limited to the institutional church; it encompasses the church. It includes families, schools, nations, and all institutions—wherever Christ's gospel and biblical law apply, namely, *across the face of the earth*. All people need the saving power of Christ. Therefore, all their relationships and institutions need the saving power of Christ's gospel. As Christians work out the implications of their faith over time, the kingdom continues to develop. God's pre-resurrection kingdom never fully replaces Satan's earthly kingdom, but it will overcome most of it.

The whole loaf is going to be leavened; the final maturity comes at the day of judgment. What does "whole loaf" mean, if not the whole world?

For further study: Ps. 89; 102:13-22; 138:4-5; Isa. 11:9; 42:1-10.

Question 57
Didn't Christ's Kingdom Begin before the Crucifixion?

If I cast out devils by the Spirit of God, then the kingdom of God is come unto you (Matthew 12:28).

The parallel passage in Luke is even more interesting: **"But if I with the *finger* of God cast out devils, no doubt the kingdom of God is come upon you"** (11:20). Jesus continued to cast out devils, thereby announcing the arrival of His kingdom. The apostles possessed the same ability, indicating the continuing power of God's kingdom over His enemy, Satan.

The kingdom began with a display of *spiritual power*. But this spiritual power had *implications for society*. It meant a reduction in the power and influence of Satan, as in the case of the converted Ephesian magicians who brought their books together and burned them, valued at 50,000 pieces of silver (Acts 19:19)—a huge sum in the first century, A.D. (Judas betrayed Christ for 30 pieces.) **"So mightily grew the word of God and prevailed"** (Acts 19:20). The emphasis on *prevailing*, on *overcoming*, is basic to the Book of Acts.

The early apostles were invading Satan's kingdom. Satan now occupies land as a *squatter*. We have the responsibility of casting his fellow demons out of people, and *casting his influence out of society*. There may not *seem* to be many demon-possessed people, but *demon-possessed cultures are everywhere*. Where God's word is rejected as the proper way of life, for whatever reason, there we find a form of demonic influence.

Questionable Answer

"The kingdom began with Jesus' ministry. But this kingdom was interrupted with His crucifixion. The kingdom which operates today is a spiritual kingdom only, not the external, civil kingdom which was prophesied in the Old Testament."

My Reply: If the kingdom *has come*, which is what Jesus said, then how could it have been cut off by His crucifixion? Throughout the New Testament, the kingdom is discussed in terms of the leaven principle: growth, maturity, expansion. There is never any discussion of possible sharp breaks, either as a result of Christ's crucifixion or because of some discontinuous break prior to the return of Christ to set up a millennial kingdom. What is always pictured by Jesus is a kingdom marked by *continuity*.

What are we to do as members of His kingdom? We are to preach the gospel and display the fruits of righteousness. We are to serve as salt in a savorless age, to serve as lights in a dark age, and to serve as ambassadors of a growing kingdom. If we do these things well, and if God decides that the time is ripe, why shouldn't our efforts produce visible, culturally significant transformations, culture by culture? We expect the acceptance of the gospel to transform primitive tribes in the jungle. Are we so corrupted by materialistic humanism that we cannot see what changes are possible in our civilization? Aren't modern humanist nations as much in need of biblical transformation as primitive societies are? Can't the gospel work in our societies, too?

For further study: Matt. 3:2; 4:17; 10:7; 12:28; 16:28; Mark 1:15.

Question 58
Wasn't Satan Cast out of Heaven During Jesus' Earthly Ministry?

Now is the judgment of this world: now shall the prince of this world be cast out. And I, if I be lifted up from the earth, will draw all men unto me. This he said, signifying what death he should die (John 12:31-33).

Now: the time is clear. *Satan suffered a tremendous defeat at the cross*. He was cast out of heaven even *before* the crucifixion, but not before Christ's birth. He was still able to come before God and accuse Job in the Old Testament. No longer: **"And I heard a loud voice saying in heaven, Now is come salvation, and strength, and the kingdom of our God, and the power of his Christ: for the accuser of our brethren is cast down, which accused them before our God day and night"** (Revelation 12:10).

Jesus sent 70 disciples out to preach. **"And the seventy returned again with joy, saying, Lord, even the devils are subject unto us through thy name. And he said unto them, I beheld Satan as lightning fall from heaven"** (Luke 10:17-18). A major transition began when Jesus began to cast out demons, and his disciples followed His example. **"Verily I say unto you, Among them that are born of women there hath not risen a greater than John the Baptist: notwithstanding he that is least in the kingdom of heaven is greater than he"** (Matthew 11:11). Not greater ethically, but greater in culture-transforming *power*. Christ's kingdom has come in great power.

Questionable Answer

"Satan was cast out of heaven in some way, as the Bible says, in the days of Jesus. Things were different after Jesus began to cast out demons. But this proves nothing about the continuous expansion of God's kingdom on earth before Christ returns physically and intervenes to establish an earthly kingdom."

My Reply: Satan was free to roam across the face of the earth outside of Israel prior to the ministry of Jesus. He controlled the whole earth as a leaseholder. He had gained that lease from Adam when Adam placed himself covenantally under Satan. But now the second Adam had come to challenge Satan's title to the whole world. When He demonstrated the advent of His kingdom by casting out devils, Christ simultaneously proclaimed the defeat of Satan and the advent of His worldwide kingdom. From that point on, Satan was on the defensive. He still is.

Christ announced His "new world order." It was a new order based on *ethical conformity to the law of God*. First, Christ obeyed the law, and was crucified as a perfect human sacrifice for Adam's sin. Second, His disciples gained authority under God to preach the gospel and cast out demons. They also conquered in terms of their adherence to God's law—the commandments of Jesus. The kingdom of God is still advancing, wherever Christ's people preach salvation and obedience to God's law. This is what is meant by the phrase, "the whole counsel of God." Ignore God's law, and you have only partial counsel.

For further study: Matt. 12:28-29; Luke 10:17-20; John 12:31-32; 16:11; Col. 2:15; Heb. 2:14; I John 3:8.

Question 59

Isn't Faith Progressively Productive Until Christians Win?

> **And so he that had received five talents came and brought other five talents, saying, Lord, thou deliveredst unto me five talents: behold, I have gained beside them five talents more. His lord said unto him, Well done, thou good and faithful servant: thou hast been faithful over a few things, I will make thee ruler over many things: enter thou into the joy of thy lord** (Matthew 25:20-21).

The parable of the talents illustrates the essence of *positive feedback* in God's kingdom. God gives us internal and external blessings that Christ's work alone has merited. We are to multiply these gifts, in time and on earth. The very English word for our skills—"talents"—comes from this parable. The talent in Bible times was a unit of weight, generally relating to gold or silver.

The man who was given five talents by God earned 100% on the money. So did the man who had been given two talents (25:22). He, too, is praised by his lord. (This should warn us against the socialistic rhetoric of "equal starting points," or "equal opportunities." God gives unequal gifts in every area of life. What counts is how well we multiply them for His honor.) The third man was fearful and had buried his coin. His reward was judgment: the lord had his servants take the man's coin and give it to the man who now had ten. *God rewards those who perform*.

Questionable Answer

"The parable of the talents relates only to spiritual gifts. It has nothing to do with earthly capital. All Jesus meant was that a man is to multiply his spiritual capital, primarily by leading people to faith in Christ."

My Reply: Most of Jesus' parables were spoken in agricultural or monetary terms. They were "pocketbook parables." He did not speak to the masses in the language of theological disputation. He spoke to them in the language they understood.

The parable of the talents teaches unmistakably that no matter what skill or gift you have received from God, you are supposed to put it to good use. It should earn a positive rate of return (25:27). You will be held responsible on judgment day. *The period of responsible action before the Lord returns* is to be redeemed (bought back). It is to be productive, in every sense of the word. Men are to gain skills of exercising good judgment. After all, who received the talent of the man who was judged? The person who had been given the greatest amount of responsibility from the first, and who had earned 100% on his "investment." From them to whom much is given, much is expected (Luke 12:47-48). As millions of Christians pursue various lines of service, the capital base of the church multiplies. This brings wealth and influence over time. But many Christians reject Christ's teaching about culture-transforming Christian labor because they have no confidence in their own talents or God's law.

For further study: Lev. 26:3; Deut. 8:18; 15:6; 28:1-14; Ps. 67:6; Prov. 3:33; 10:22; Isa. 47:17-19; Mark 10:29-30; I Tim. 4:8.

Question 60

How Can Satan Rule the World if Power Comes from Righteousness?

Blessed are the meek: for they shall inherit the earth (Matthew 5:5).

Who are the meek? Those people who are *meek before God*. They are not those who are meek before Satan. They are also not those who are ethically weak. They acknowledge their total dependence on God, and their need to obey His revealed word. But they recognize that it is this meekness and obedience that bring ultimate victory, in time and on earth.

Where is the arena of conflict? On earth. When does this drama take place? Before the end of time. What is the prize of the conflict? Control over the earth. Of course, it is more than this, for what does it profit a man if he gains the whole earth and loses his soul (Mark 8:36, 37)? But it is difficult to avoid the implications of this verse: *inheriting the earth* is what Christ offered as the *incentive*.

The religion of Satan is a *power religion*. Satan sees all conflict as a conflict involving a power struggle. God sees the struggle as *ethical*. Whose name do we honor, man's or God's? This is the chief ethical question. **"Some trust in chariots, and some in horses: but we will remember the name of the LORD our God"** (Psalm 20:7). **"There is no king saved by the multitude of an host: a mighty man is not delivered by much strength. An horse is a vain thing for safety: neither shall he deliver any by his great strength"** (Psalm 33:16-17).

Questionable Answer

"The meek person does not seek power. He does not try to lord it over other people. He goes meekly about his affairs, not demanding anything from others. He inherits the whole earth immediately after the return of Jesus to establish His earthly rule."

My Reply: Can Mr. Christian Milquetoast learn overnight how to run a business, command an army, run a Congressional staff, be the president of a university, be the chairman of a research laboratory, take responsibility for operating a $300 million investment trust, be the editor of a newspaper, or any of a thousand other tasks that demand *forceful leadership*? Isn't the development of leadership a long-term process?

The question is: Before whom will a man be meek? If he is meek before God, God says he will inherit the earth. If he is confident in his rebellion against God, he will lose both the earth and his own soul. Satan wasn't meek before God; he will perish under the judgment of God. Meekness is what we call an inescapable concept. It's not a question of "meekness vs. confidence." It's a question of *meekness before whom or what?*

Meekness is progressive. We learn to humble ourselves before the Lord. We learn to conform our dreams and our actions before God. But because meekness is progressive, *inheriting the earth is also progressive.* Self-discipline brings authority. But this authority is not to be confined to the institutional church. It is *comprehensive authority*, for the gospel's effects are comprehensive.

For further study: Ps. 37; 110; Isa. 45:8-25; 49:5-12.

Question 61
Aren't Christians Supposed to Crush Satan?

And the God of peace shall bruise Satan under your feet shortly. The grace of our Lord Jesus Christ be with you. Amen (Romans 16:20).

Paul wrote to the church at Rome that in a short period of time, they would see Satan bruised under their feet. Obviously, Paul was speaking figuratively. They did not as a group collectively step on the head of a physical serpent. What they did was to begin to participate in *a collective, church-wide battering of Satan's kingdom*. This was yet another stage of the fulfilment of that crucial prophecy to Satan: **"And I will put enmity between thee and the woman, and between thy seed and her seed; it shall bruise thy head, and thou shalt bruise his heel"** (Genesis 3:15).

The warfare between Christ and Satan is ethical. As the two armies meet each other on the battlefield, the Christians have access to the critically important training manual for ethical war: the Bible. This gives Christ's forces an overwhelming potential advantage. *The problem arises when His troops refuse to honor the specific commands in God's ethical battle plan*. His people are driven from the field repeatedly, for they lose skirmishes. Why do they lose? Because they reject the explicit teachings of God concerning Himself, man, law, the church, the family, the civil government, and all other areas of responsibility that the Bible deals with. But the church at Rome could rest confidently. They knew that they would experience a victory.

Questionable Answer

"The bruising of Satan's head is a spiritual bruising. God's people do not actually conquer Satan's visible kingdom. They do conquer his temptations of them as individuals. But this has nothing to do with cultural phenomena."

My Reply: If we can conquer Satan's individual temptations, then how do we do it? By adhering to God's law, and relying on His grace. But if we steadily bring ourselves under the discipline of God's law as individuals, and also as members of God's institutional church, why does this progressive victory over Satan have to stop at the doors of our homes and our churches? What restrains us from bringing more of the world under His dominion by means of an expansion of our responsibilities as individuals and as church members? Why are we unable to experience the same sort of success outside the home and the church? What about in education? What about in all the other areas of life? Why is God's law, coupled with God's grace, incapable of progressively sanctifying ("setting apart" through ethical conformity to God) the whole society? Is there anything in the Bible which tells us that what works for us as individuals and church members will invariably fail when attempted by godly men and women in other institutions? Are Christians competent in the home and church, but inevitably incompetent everywhere else? Why should Christians suffer from a cultural inferiority complex? Is our gospel impotent?

For further study: Rom. 8:37; Eph. 6:10-13; Jas. 4:7; I Pet. 5:8-9; I John 4:4; 5:4.

Question 62
What Can Possibly Interrupt Christ's Dominion?

I saw in the night visions, and, behold, one like the Son of man came with the clouds of heaven, and came to the Ancient of days, and they brought him near before him. And there was given him dominion, and glory, and a kingdom, that all people, nations, and languages, should serve him: his dominion is an everlasting dominion, which shall not pass away, and his kingdom that which shall not be destroyed (Daniel 7:13-14).

Who received this everlasting kingdom? Obviously, Jesus Christ. This probably took place upon His entry into heaven after His death on the cross (Luke 23:43), for He announced to His disciples *after* His resurrection but *before* His ascension: **"All power is given unto me in heaven and in earth"** (Matthew 28:18).

What happened to this dominion? Is it still in force? Are the laws governing it consistent throughout Christ's reign, until His return on the day of final judgment? We have seen in earlier sections of this book that Christ said His commandments are binding forever. But if they are still binding, and men are to achieve success or failure in terms of them, can we legitimately believe that we can abandon our commitment to His commandments and expand the visible sovereignty of His jurisdiction? Can't we actually trace the decline of influence of the church in Western culture since 1870 with its abandonment of His law?

Questionable Answer

"Christ's everlasting dominion appears in three stages: 1) the kingdom of heaven, which Christ announced during His ministry, and which was begun definitively after the resurrection, and lasted until Pentecost (Acts 2), 50 days after His ascension (Acts 1); 2) the church age (kingdom of God), from Pentecost until the Rapture; and 3) a revival of the kingdom of heaven, during Christ's personal 1000-year reign. Old Testament law is binding only in stages one and three. It does not produce dominion in stage 2, the church age."

My Reply: If the so-called "church age" were really a period in which biblical law is not applicable, and if it were really a "great parenthesis," unknown to the Old Testament prophets and set up by God only because Israel rejected Christ as Messiah, then *what happened to the first kingdom?* If the kingdom of heaven (Matthew) isn't the same as the kingdom of God spoken of elsewhere, did Christ receive *two separate kingdoms*, the second which began in Acts 8 (or 28), and the other which was given after His death, but postponed for over 1900 years when the Jews rejected Christ's rule and the church age began? *How does an "everlasting" kingdom get interrupted 50 days later* (Pentecost: Acts 2)?

Why do the parables of Matthew 13 describe a progressive continuity of development, if there are so many discontinuities? Why are the "laws of growth" for wheat in one era useless for wheat in another era? And could today's lack of growth be due to Christianity's abandonment of God's laws?

For further study: Luke 9:27; 10:9-11; 11:20; 17:21; 21:31; 22:29.

Question 63
Isn't Christ's Kingdom in This World?

Jesus answered, My kingdom is not of this world: if my kingdom were of this world, then would my servants fight, that I should not be delivered to the Jews: but now is my kingdom not from hence (John 18:36).

Here is a frequently misinterpreted passage. Pilate had asked Jesus: **"Am I a Jew? Thine own nation and the chief priests have delivered thee unto me: what hast thou done?"** (18:35). Christ was responding to Pilate's implication that he was sovereign over Christ because he was the representative of Rome, which in turn was sovereign over Israel. By implication, Christ was simply another political or religious troublemaker who had come before the seat of Roman power.

Not so, answered Christ. He did not deny that He had a kingdom; on the contrary, He affirmed it. His response did not affirm Pilate's assertion of implicit authority over Christ. Christ's kingdom was not of this world. What did this mean? It meant that His kingdom *did not originate* in this world. The "of" denotes *place of origin* and/or *location of authority*. Christ did *not* say that His kingdom is not *in* this world; He said that it was not *of* this world. In short, Christ asserted, Pilate had no ultimate jurisdiction over Him just because Rome had temporary visible power over Israel.

Notice also the word "now": "*now* **is my kingdom not from hence**." But this says nothing about the day of judgment, or even the day of His resurrection.

Questionable Answer

"Christ's kingdom did not originate in this world. At the time of the crucifixion He had no earthly supporters who would fight for him. But in His millennial reign, when He appears physically to rule with a rod of iron, His kingdom will be of this world—a link between heaven and earth. But today, in the church age, His kingdom is not of this world, so we are not required to fight to defend Him and His reputation. We are not to attempt the construction of a Christian kingdom."

My Reply: The question we need to have answered is this one: When did, does, or will the "now" be removed from Christ's sentence? When will He be able to announce that His kingdom is now of this world, because its place of origin—heaven—has come down to earth? Clearly, this will take place after the final judgment. But will it take place before? Or has it taken place already?

Jesus announced at the last supper: **"And I appoint unto you a kingdom, as my Father hath appointed unto me; that ye may eat and drink at my table in my kingdom, and sit on thrones judging the twelve tribes of Israel"** (Luke 22:29-30). He announced after His resurrection, **"All power is given unto me in heaven and in earth"** (Matthew 28:18). Where? In heaven and in earth. Here was the fusion. *Now* His kingdom *is* of this world. Now His followers *do* fight for His honor, for they serve a risen Lord who has demonstrated His power over death. His kingdom is now visible in this world through His people.

For further study: Rom. 14:17; Col. 1:13; 4:11; I Thess. 2:12; Heb. 12:28; Rev. 1:5-6.

Question 64

Doesn't the New Testament Teach That Christians Are Powerful?

The eyes of your understanding being enlightened; that ye may know what is the hope of his calling, and what the riches of the glory of his inheritance in the saints, and what is the exceeding greatness of his power to us-ward who believe, according to the working of his mighty power (Ephesians 1:18-19).

Christ has delivered power to His church. He has also granted us a *vast inheritance*. Why don't we see this? Because we are blind to God's word. Christ has not given us the full inheritance, for the world is still in sin, and so are we, but we have been given a *down payment*, what Paul called an "earnest" a few sentences earlier (v. 14). We are to recognize the magnitude of both His power and our inheritance, in time and on earth, as we progressively work out our salvation with fear and trembling. How extensive is Christ's power? God gave power to Him "**when he raised him from the dead, and set him at his own right hand in the heavenly places, far above all principality, and power, and might, and dominion, and every name that is named, not only in this world, but also in that which is to come: and hath put all things under his feet, and gave him to be the head over all things to the church, which is his body, the fulness of him that filleth all in all**" (vv. 20-23). If this isn't comprehensive power, what is? As church members, we are commanded by the Lord of all power, who was victorious at Calvary.

Questionable Answer

"Christ possesses all power as a result of His resurrection victory over Satan. The church, however, has no means of appropriating this power in time and on earth. Christ grants to the church power over the second death. He grants it the sacraments. But He reserves power for Himself, which the church will not be able to use until after the Second Coming."

My Reply: Why did Paul spend so much space discussing such comprehensive power, and the inheritance, and Christ's down payment "to us-ward," if God has chosen never to grant Christ's people the visible, earthly power commensurate (though of course not identical) with the power that He granted to Christ, the head of the church? Ephesians 1 discusses God's predestination of every member of His church, the magnitude of God's power and wealth, the headship of Christ over the church, and Christ's comprehensive dominion over all creation in His perfect humanity (He enjoyed this authority in His divinity before the resurrection). Where is our dominion?

If the church is His body, **"the fulness of him that filleth all in all,"** why is it so pathetically unfilled? Is the kingdom forever doomed to be weak in comparison to Satan's troops? Why is that majestic power which was *in principle* transferred to the church from the beginning incapable of becoming visible, in time and on earth? Or have Christians simply ignored God's law? In short, why do so many Christians refuse to exercise the power the gospel has provided? Why are they so faithless?

For further study: I Cor. 4:20; II Tim. 1:7; Rev. 1:6; 2:26-28; 5:10.

Question 65

Aren't Christians Supposed to Execute Judgment?

> **Do ye not know that the saints shall judge the world? And if the world shall be judged by you, are ye unworthy to judge the smallest matters? Know ye not that we shall judge angels? How much more things that pertain to this life?** (I Corinthians 6:2-3).

Paul warned the Corinthian church not to enter into courtroom disputes with each other in front of pagan judges. He told them to set up church courts for that purpose. In other words, they needed training in settling legal disputes. Did this mean that Christians are always to limit their quest for judgment to church courts?

If it meant this, then why did Paul bring up the issue of judging the world and the angels? If Christians are supposed to limit themselves strictly to church court trials, how are they to obtain the wisdom to be able to judge the world? What does it mean, "judge the world"?

The whole world is under Jesus Christ's authority (Matthew 28:18). He is steadily bringing it under His visible sovereignty through the spread of the gospel. As more people profess faith in Him, and seek progressively to govern their actions in terms of biblical law, His kingdom expands. As we become proficient in judging our personal actions, and then in judging the actions of other Christians in church courts, we thereby gain the experience necessary for judging matters outside the institutional church.

Questionable Answer

"Christians have no power, right, or need to judge other people's actions. The Bible says plainly, 'Judge not, that ye be not judged.' It is not our task to establish a theocracy."

My Reply: **"Judge not, that ye be not judged"** (Matthew 7:1). But Paul said that we *will* judge. How can we reconcile this apparent contradiction? By examining the next verse: **"For with what judgment ye judge, ye shall be judged: and with what measure ye mete, it shall be measured to you again"** (7:2). Thus, if a person wishes to place himself under the jurisdiction of God's kingdom, he must be ready to *judge* sin and be *judged by* biblical law. If he wants that benefit, then he must judge in terms of biblical law, for with what standard he judges others, he will in turn be judged. Thus, *to refrain from judging in terms of biblical law is to place oneself under the administration of some other system of law*. We must use biblical law.

Christians have adopted a rival law structure in the modern world. They have refused to bring judgment on themselves, either personally or ecclesiastically, in terms of God's law. They have abandoned the courts to pagan judges. They have not become proficient in enacting civil legislation. The result? God-hating pagans have imposed their laws over Christians. Christians are today being judged by an alien law structure. This will continue until they recapture the institutions of power. Either we judge evil, or evil men will judge us.

For further study: Ex. 23:1-8; Ps. 119:34, 53, 66, 73, 97-104, 130, 163; Prov. 17:15; Dan. 7:22; Zech. 8:16; John 7:24; Phil. 1:9-11.

Question 66
Why Shouldn't Christians Become Civil Rulers and Enforce God's Law?

For rulers are not a terror to good works, but to the evil. Wilt thou then not be afraid of the power? Do that which is good, and thou shalt have praise of the same. For he is the minister of God to thee for good. But if thou do that which is evil, be afraid; for he beareth not the sword in vain: for he is the minister of God, a revenger to execute wrath upon him that doeth evil (Romans 13:3-4).

God has ordained the institution of civil government as a monopolistic agency which imposes physical sanctions against evil-doers. The civil magistrate is His minister of vengeance. Civil government is an inescapable concept. It is never a question of civil government vs. no civil government. It is always a question of *which kind* of civil government. Pure anarchy is not a possibility. Someone or some agency will always bear the sword of physical judgment.

Civil government is not supposed to make men good. It is not an agency of regeneration. It is *ministerial*. Thus, its task is to *restrain certain kinds of **public** evil acts* by all people, regenerate or unregenerate. Its task is to be a terror to those who would commit evil acts.

How should a civil government define publicly punishable evil acts? *By what standard?* Clearly, by God's revealed law. Which citizens are best equipped to make this determination? Humanists? Or Christians?

Questionable Answer

"Paul says that Christians are not to seek vengeance (Romans 12:19). Thus, it is the responsibility of the Christian to obey the civil government, not to seek to take it over. Christians have no responsibility to bear the sword of vengeance."

My Reply: Paul wrote a few lines earlier: **"Dearly beloved, avenge not yourselves, but rather give place unto wrath: for it is written, Vengeance is mine; I will repay, saith the Lord"** (Romans 12:19). The Bible was not originally divided into chapters. Thus, these words give us the proper foundation for interpreting the passage dealing with the civil magistrate.

Vengeance belongs to God. The civil magistrate is God's ordained agent of vengeance. Thus, he who serves as a civil magistrate performs the function which is prohibited to individuals who are acting on their own. Private citizens aren't allowed to "take the law into their own hands." But the passage says nothing about Christians not being allowed to *take the law into God's own hands*, as His lawful agents. There is not a word against Christians serving as civil magistrates. On the contrary, the whole passage implies that we should strive to improve the enforcement of civil law by striving to change all civil laws to conform to the specific details of biblical law. This would promote the progressive sanctification of the civil government. Wouldn't the enforcement of God's civil law be an improvement? Wouldn't it externalize God's kingdom?

For further study: Lev. 19:15; Deut. 4:5-8; 17:18-20; Ps. 2:10-12; 101:5-8; Prov. 14:34; 16:12.

Question 67
Doesn't the Bible Require an Appeals Court?

Casting down imaginations, and every high thing that exalteth itself against the knowledge of God, and bringing into captivity every thought to the obedience of Christ; and having in a readiness to revenge all disobedience, when your obedience is fulfilled (II Corinthians 10:5-6).

There is a *progressive sanctifying of the creation*, from the heart to the society at large. First, there is regeneration, when we receive the mind of Christ (I Corinthians 2:16). We cast down evil and vain imaginations that are in opposition to the knowledge God provides of Himself. This establishes our presuppositions on the revelation found in the Bible. Next, we bring our thoughts captive to Christ. This is *intellectual self-discipline*, and the standard of success is the Bible.

Having achieved this in our personal lives, we then apply our wisdom to other areas: home, church, school, business, and civil government. The New American Standard Version translates verse 6 as: **"we are ready to punish all disobedience, whenever your obedience is complete."** When the elders of the church at Corinth have at last decided to enforce biblical law, then they can call in Paul and other elders to serve as outside judges in cases where disobedience still prevails among unruly members. Church sanctification is progressive; as men discipline themselves, they can call in godly judges for more serious problems.

Questionable Answer

"This has to do with church government, not civil or any other kind of government. Paul was speaking only of the rule of the Holy Spirit in the church."

My Reply: Paul introduced this section with the words, **"For the weapons of our warfare are not carnal, but mighty through God to the pulling down of strong holds"** (v. 4). What he says is almost precisely the opposite of what modern Bible teachers say. It is the spiritual weapon which is mighty, not the carnal. Our modern teachers are too much bedazzled by the *power religion* of the pagans. What is weak is power religion.

First, regeneration. Next, intellectual discipline in terms of the Bible. Next, a willingness of church leaders to obey biblical law personally (Matthew 7:1-2), and enforce it inside the church. Then God provides an appeals court, with higher judges who are ready to support local elders in their enforcement of biblical law. This is how Christ's earthly kingdom is expanded in the church. But it is no different in any other governmental unit. This hierarchical appeals court system is what Moses imposed over Israel (Exodus 18).

Where Christians seek to understand God's law, and agree to conform themselves to it, they are ready to exercise dominion in every area of life. This process begins in the local church, but it was never intended by God to be confined there forever.

For further study: Gen. 12:3; 49:10; Ps. 46:10; 65:2; 66:4; Zech. 8:20-23; 14:8-9, 16; Mal. 1:11.

Question 68

Won't the Resurrection Take Place after the Millennium?

But every man in his own order: Christ the firstfruits; afterward they that are Christ's at his coming. Then cometh the end, when he shall have delivered up the kingdom to God, even the Father; when he shall have put down all rule and all authority and power (I Corinthians 15:23-24).

The firstfruits were offered at Pentecost in the Old Testament. They are the first fruits offered of each man's productivity. Christ was not only the Passover but also the firstfruits. He was the first offering. We will be next. Our resurrection is assured.

The parable of the wheat and the tares informs us that *continuity* of development is basic to the kingdom of God. There is no separation of the wheat and the tares until the end of time. This passage informs us that there is only one resurrection after Christ's: our resurrection. "***Then* cometh the end.**"

Those who believe in a 1,000-year personal, physical reign of Christ on earth have to argue that the word "then" covers at least 1,000 years (and maybe 1,007). They say this in order to make their prophecy system work. But you would never postulate a 1,000-year "then" if you had read only this passage. We will be resurrected, and then comes the final judgment, the end of time. This comes *after* Christ has put down all the opposition. How will He do this? Through His people, who exercise dominion.

Questionable Answer

"The inability of the church to exercise authority without Jesus' physical presence on earth is obvious. There is no progress culturally. Things are getting worse. They have gotten worse in a straight line since the end of the first century, A.D. Christ will not put down His enemies through us."

My Reply: "**I can do all things through Christ which strengtheneth me**" (Philippians 4:13). If Paul could do all things through Christ, then what prevents Christ's church from extending Christ's rule on earth, in response to God's dominion covenant (Genesis 1:27-28; 9:1-7)? Did Paul seek to mislead us about the spiritual power of God? Did he want us to lose faith in the power imparted by the Holy Spirit, coupled with God's law?

Clearly, the history of the church has had its ups and downs. But we are far better off today than in the first century. Anyone can afford his own printed Bible. We have the history of creeds to show us where misinterpretations arose, and how the church dealt with them. We have communications satellites. We have great per capita wealth, the product (initially) of the Protestant work ethic. We have more responsibilities, of course, but clearly we have more influence and power. And what we lack can be overcome, if and when we return to faith in the *comprehensive power of the gospel*. If we deny that God's kingdom principles can change the world, haven't we thereby said that these principles are culturally impotent?

For further study: Isa. 56:3-8; 59:19-21; 62:1-12; 66:7-23; Zech. 14:20-21.

Question 69

Won't Men Live Longer as God's Kingdom Progresses?

> **For he must reign, till he hath put all enemies under his feet. The last enemy that shall be destroyed is death** (I Corinthians 15:25-26).

The parable of the wheat and the tares stresses continuity. So do the other parables of the kingdom in Matthew 13. But can we believe in continuity—progressive sanctification—in the area of *biology*? Yes, death will be put down, once and for all, at the end of time. But this is a radically *discontinuous* event. If we expect progressive sanctification culturally, economically, and so forth, as God's blessing for the enforcement of His law, shouldn't we also expect to see a steady lengthening of human life spans, as a testimony ("earnest") of the coming conquest of death? Do biblical ethics and long life go together?

"Honor thy father and thy mother: that thy days may be long upon the land which the LORD thy God giveth thee" (Exodus 20:12). Paul cited this passage and remarked that this was the first of the commandments with a promise attached to it (Ephesians 6:2). This law and its promise still hold.

Will long life be universal, in response to the expansion of God's kingdom? This is what Isaiah prophesied: **"There shall be no more thence an infant of days, nor an old man that hath not filled his days: for the child shall die an hundred years old; but the sinner being an hundred years old shall be accursed"** (65:20). Biblical ethics and long life *do* go together.

Questionable Answer

"These long life spans are a product of Christ's miraculous intervention during the millennial reign. This reign is personal and physical, and requires us to believe in a discontinuous kingdom event: Christ's second coming and the resurrection of believers."

My Reply: The reduction of life spans from Noah's era until Joshua's day, from over 900 years to three score and ten (average), took several centuries to complete. This was not a discontinuous process. It was gradual. Thus, when the Bible promises an increase of life spans this side of the final judgment (Isaiah spoke of sinners living and dying during this period), it is prophesying a gradual return to what men once experienced before the flood. Why shouldn't we believe in continuity?

If we are told by Isaiah to believe in a continuous increase in life in response to an increase in ethical self-discipline under God, and in response to the governing of human institutions by biblical law, then why is it so difficult to believe in something "minor," such as economic growth, or technological development, or more justice in civil government, or a reduction in the number of wars? If man's very body can and will experience a continuous increase in life expectancy, why not also a progressive healing of other aspects of man's life—things that are seemingly far less fixed than life expectancy? *Earthly victory is coming!*

Why do so many Christians preach a coming earthly defeat?

For further study: Ex. 20:12; Deut. 5:16; Ps. 91:16; Prov. 3:2; Eph. 6:3.

Question 70
Doesn't Christ's Kingdom Expand over Time?

Thy kingdom come. Thy will be done in earth, as it is in heaven (Matthew 6:10).

We are to pray for God's kingdom to come. But Christ said that when the disciples saw Him casting out demons that they would know that the kingdom had already come (Luke 11:20). So why are we to pray, **"Thy kingdom come"**?

We must understand the biblical triad: *definitive, progressive*, and *final*. God gives us definitive sanctification when we are regenerated—Christ's righteousness imputed to us. We work out the implications of this definitive sanctification throughout our lives (Philippians 2:12b). Then on the day of judgment we receive our final, perfect sanctification which had been granted to us *in principle* at the moment of our conversion.

The kingdom came, and the final kingdom will come. In the meantime, we as Christians are to work out *historically* the implications of what God gave to us definitively with Christ's ministry—definitive, progressive (historical), and final.

How do we judge our success in our efforts to develop Christ's kingdom principles, *before* the final judgment? By comparing God's law to what we have built by using God's law. This is why Christ also required that we pray, **"Thy will be done in earth, as it is in heaven."** God's kingdom is not marked by Christ's physical presence on earth for 1,000 years; His kingdom is marked by *our progressive application of God's law on earth*.

Questionable Answer

"This prayer was a prayer of saints in the kingdom of heaven, meaning the Jewish kingdom. It is not to be prayed by church members, who belong to the kingdom of God, a completely different kingdom age."

My Reply: "**Thy kingdom come.**" How many kingdoms? One kingdom. So we are to pray for its full development historically—the complete manifestation of God's will, exercised on earth by His people. The prayer is *ethical*. It refers to *law*, which is *God's will* for those who live on earth.

Nevertheless, God's kingdom is manifested in power. We do not seek power as such; we pray for God's will to be applied on earth as it is in heaven. But Christ announced His total power in heaven and on earth. His power was based on His performance of the requirements of God's law. In short, He received total power because He conformed totally to God's ethical requirements for mankind. His *perfect humanity* entitled Him to *perfect power*.

As we conform ourselves progressively to His will, we also increase our power, for God increases our authority over human affairs. As His people seek God's will on earth, and as they discipline themselves and those under their lawful jurisdiction by the categories of biblical law, we should expect to see *progressive blessings* and *progressive responsibility*, both internal and external, personal and social (Deuteronomy 28:1-14).

For further study: Dan. 2:34-35, 44-45; 7:13-27; Amos 9:11-13; Rom. 11:11-32.

Question 71
Doesn't God Want His "Heirs" to Inherit Everything?

> For the promise, that he should be the heir of the world, was not to Abraham, or to his seed, through the law, but through the righteousness of faith (Romans 4:13).

Abraham was given a promise: he would inherit the *world,* through his seed. He would see his name established throughout the world. **"I will bless them that bless thee, and curse him that curseth thee: and in thee shall all families of the earth be blessed"** (Genesis 12:3). But Paul said that this promise was secured by Abraham's faith.

Do Christians believe in this promise? They believe that they will experience the resurrection. In this way, they will become heirs. But Abraham saw the fulfilment of this promise differently. God told him that his seed would multiply astronomically, and that his heirs would inherit the whole land of Canaan (Genesis 15:5-7). By faith, he appropriated this promise (15:6). But it was to be a *visible* expansion. God made the promise in the language of *measurement*—indeed, beyond measurement (16:10), as the stars of heaven or the sand of the sea.

Abraham did not expect overnight fulfilment. It could not be accomplished. First, he needed an heir. Only then could he expect the fulfilment of the promise. He expected lineal and linear growth over time. Why do modern Christians so often expect victory only after death or the resurrection?

Questionable Answer

"Paul changed the focus of the promise. It is spiritual heirship that matters today. We are not to expect progressive population growth among Christians, or progressive economic growth among Christian nations. We should expect only increased spiritual insight and personal self-discipline among Christians."

My Reply: Abraham expected all these things. He knew about self-discipline. He was the commander of a large household. He was a successful military strategist. His faith was counted for righteousness. He was no primitive dweller of the desert. He was an educated, wise man. But he expected *economic growth* and *population growth* to accompany the growth of spiritual insight on the part of his heirs. Why? Because God had expressed the promise in terms of external blessings. God said the same thing to Moses and the people of Israel (Deuteronomy 28:1-14).

Why *shouldn't* personal self-discipline, honest business dealings, insights into the true nature of man, thrift, future-orientation, gifts from God, access to the Bible, regular preaching, regular tithing, six days of labor instead of five each week, respect for the sabbath, covenantal marriages, and experience in bringing up large households result in economic growth, intellectual growth, and the progressive expansion of personal and covenantal responsibility and dominion? Get an answer. Soon.

For further study: Lev. 26:3-13; Deut. 28:1-14; Josh. 1:7-8; Ps. 1:1-3; 119:1-2, 165.

Question 72
Didn't the Prophets Foresee the Church Age?

> **Yea, and all the prophets from Samuel and those that follow after, as many as have spoken, have likewise foretold of these days (Acts 3:24).**

Peter was quite specific: *all* the prophets from Samuel onward foretold the church age. This means that God gave revelation to Old Testament believers concerning the great era of the gospel of Jesus Christ. Peter, in the very inauguration of the church, referred back to these Old Testament prophecies.

We are told by dispensationalists that the church age was a "great parenthesis" for the Old Testament prophets, that they knew nothing about it. Yet here is Peter telling his Hebrew listeners precisely the opposite. In this passage, he was condemning them for their murder of the Lord. He was telling them that they were morally responsible for having failed to recognize in the ministry of Jesus the fulfilment of prophecy. Notice also that he referred to **"these days"** as the time in which the Old Testament prophecies have been fulfilled.

The doctrine of the "great parenthesis"—that our era, the church age, had not been planned from the beginning by God and even foretold by God through His prophets—is a false doctrine. Yet this is perhaps the most important of all doctrines in the dispensationalist system. How, then, can the traditional dispensational system be maintained? Let us have hope that the wonderful prophecies of future victory on earth will be fulfilled, as promised, in the church age!

Questionable Answer

"Peter was preaching in a transition era. He was still offering the kingdom to Israel. If Israel had repented as a nation, Christ would have immediately returned to set up the millennial kingdom."

My Reply: Yes, this was a transitional period. Jerusalem had not yet been destroyed. That's why Peter and the author of the Epistle to the Hebrews spoke of **"these last days"** (Hebrews 1:2). But they also relate **"these days"** to their era, meaning our era, meaning the church age, meaning the *kingdom age*.

Christ had promised that in that generation, they would see Jerusalem surrounded and taken by their enemies (Luke 21:20-24). This was not a prophecy concerning some future Jerusalem, for the parallel passage in Matthew 24 reports that Christ warned: **"Verily I say unto you, This generation shall not pass, till all these things be fulfilled"** (Matthew 24:34). He had already told them that the kingdom would be taken away from them and given—not *might* be taken away, but would be: **"Therefore I say unto you, The kingdom of God shall be taken from you, and given to a nation bringing forth the fruits thereof"** (Matthew 21:43). It was a *prophecy*. Had Jesus made a mistake? No; there was no possibility that Israel might go on as before until the last judgment, without the advent of the church age. Peter was making the offer of salvation to the Jews in the church age.

Once Jerusalem was judged in 70 A.D., the **"last days"** spoken of by the Apostles ended. The transition ended. But the church age (kingdom age) had been in operation for 40 years by 70 A.D.

For further study: Matt. 12:28; 16:28; Rom. 14:17; Col. 1:13; I Thess. 2:12; Heb. 12:28; I Pet. 2:9; Rev. 1:6.

Question 73
Didn't David Foresee the Church Age?

For David is not ascended into the heavens: but he saith himself, The LORD said unto my Lord, Sit thou on my right hand, until I make thy foes thy footstool. Therefore let all the house of Israel know assuredly, that God hath made that same Jesus, whom ye have crucified, both Lord and Christ (Acts 2:34-36).

Peter called David **"a prophet"** (Acts 2:30). **"Therefore being a prophet, and knowing that God had sworn with an oath to him, that of the fruit of his loins, according to the flesh, he would raise up Christ to sit on his throne; he** *seeing this before spake of the resurrection of Christ,* **that his soul was not left in hell, neither his flesh did see corruption"** (2:30, 31). Peter proclaimed Christ's Lordship to the Jews, calling them to repentance. He did this just after he had cited the tongues of Pentecost as the fulfilment of Joel's prophecy.

Could anything be clearer? Peter believed that the offer to the Jews to repent was still open (just as we do today), and that they would have to enter the church of Jesus Christ, which had begun that morning (just as we say today). The church age had unmistakably begun that morning. The birthday of the church was the morning of Pentecost! Yet here was Peter, proclaiming Christ as Savior and Lord to the Jews. Then he called them to repentance (2:38-40). *He called them to join the church of Jesus Christ!*

Questionable Answer

"Well, then, the church must have started after Acts 2. Maybe it started in Acts 9, when Paul was called. Or maybe it started in Acts 28, when Paul ceased to preach directly to the Jews. But the prophets of Israel never foresaw the church."

My Reply: This has been the response of the "ultra-dispensationalists," some of whom date the church at Acts 9, and some at Acts 28. They have seen the untenable position that traditional dispensationalists are attempting to defend. They see that the prophecies cited by Peter in Acts 2 were fulfilled at Pentecost, and so they argue that Pentecost had nothing to do with the church age, the "great parenthesis" which no Old Testament prophet forecast. Pentecost took place in the Jewish dispensation.

The **"last days"** were taking place in the *Jewish* dispensation which overlapped **"these days,"** the *church age*. The proper answer should be clear by now. The prophets of the Old Testament looked forward to the church, and they prophesied concerning it. Prophecy was still being fulfilled in our era, the church age, meaning "the kingdom age."

But if "the clock of prophecy stopped" at Christ's ascension, then not a single prophecy has been fulfilled since then, and therefore *every dispensational book claiming that **any** event after Christ's ascension is a fulfilment of prophecy is utterly inconsistent with this most crucial of all dispensational doctrines.*

For further study: Acts 2:16; 13:32-48; 15:14-19; Rom. 9:23-33; Heb. 8:6-12.

Question 74
Didn't Moses Foresee the Church Age?

But ye are a chosen generation, a royal priesthood, an holy nation, a peculiar people; that ye should shew forth the praises of him who hath called you out of darkness into his marvelous light: Which in time past were not a people, but are now the people of God: which had not obtained mercy, but now have obtained mercy (I Peter 2:9-10).

Peter wrote this to Gentiles who were never part of God's chosen people. The prophecy of the kingdom of priests is from Exodus 19:5, 6: **"Now therefore, if ye will obey my voice indeed, and keep my covenant, then ye shall be a peculiar treasure unto me above all people: for all the earth is mine. And ye shall be unto me a kingdom of priests, and an holy nation. These are the words which thou shalt speak unto the children of Israel."**

Here is a remarkable fulfilment of prophecy. God promised the Israelites that they would eventually become a kingdom of priests, if they obeyed His law. Now Peter was telling the Gentiles that they are the heirs of this prophecy, the long-awaited fulfilment of this prophecy. The promise of God came to the Gentile church. The fulfilment of this Old Testament prophecy took place (and is still taking place) in the church age. The problem for the dispensationalist, once again, is to explain how the church age sees the fulfilment of a very specific Old Testament prophecy, if the church wasn't prophesied.

Questionable Answer

"There were two churches in the transition period between the Old Testament and the New Testament. One was a Jewish church, which Peter ministered unto, and the other was the church, the body of Christ, which Paul ministered unto. Peter wrote this epistle to the Jewish church, not to the Great Parenthesis Gentile church."

My Reply: This is the answer of the ultradispensationalists who date the church, meaning the Gentile church which was never foreseen in the Old Testament, with the advent of Paul's ministry. They proclaim two churches, one Jewish and one Gentile, to match two different kingdoms, the Jewish kingdom of heaven and the Gentile kingdom of God.

And is Christ married to two brides? Both the church and Israel are called the bride of God in the Bible. Is Christ a bigamist?

The traditional dispensationalist would have to answer differently. He would probably point to that old familiar theme, the "transitional era." This was a fulfilled prophecy in the church age, but it was not yet the church age for the Jews. But who was Peter writing to? He refers to a people who had never been the people of God. Israel had been the people of God. This prophecy must refer to Gentiles. So the church age *was* known in the Old Testament! Therefore, the key argument of dispensationalism—the Church as a "great parenthesis"—isn't true. Have you been equally misled concerning other doctrines?

For further study: Acts 7:38; Rom. 2:28-29; 10:19; 11:17-21; I Cor. 10:4; Gal. 3:8-9, 14, 29; Phil. 3:2-3; Heb. 12:22-23.

Question 75
Aren't There Two Kinds of Salvation?

> **For therefore we both labour and suffer reproach, because we trust in the living God, who is the Saviour of all men, specially of those that believe** (I Timothy 4:10).

Christ is the Savior of all men. The words are inescapable. Does this mean universal salvation? Will no man go to hell? This is what the so-called "universalists" erroneously believe.

So what do the words mean? They mean that there are *two kinds of salvation:* common and special. There are therefore *two kinds of grace:* common and special. Common grace relates to earthly life itself and the benefits associated with earthly life. Special grace relates to a man's exercise of saving faith, which is possible only because of the sovereign grace of God.

The word "save" is related to "salvation," which in turn is related to "salve." A salve is a healing ointment. This is a very good description of Christ's work at Calvary. *Christ healed the whole universe by His death.* Because of this, God did not destroy the world on the day Adam rebelled. This salve heals some men's souls and all men's environment.

This is why Christ's salvation is *comprehensive.* It affects everything, for it was designed to heal everything progressively, and finally on the day of judgment. This is why obedience to God's law brings long-term growth and progress. We live in an orderly universe—ordered by the ethical character of God.

Questionable Answer

"Jesus died to save souls. He did not die to save civilizations, or to enable His people to build one. The kingdom of God is internal, not external. It's all a Christian can do to get his own life in order, let alone the world. So that's what we should do: *let alone the world.*"

My Reply: When the Bible says that Christ is the savior of all men, *especially* of those that believe, it can mean one of two things. First, Christ saves all men from hell, but gives special blessings to those who accepted Christ during their lives. Second, it means that there are two kinds of salvation, one which heals all men's earthly environment (by God's refraining from destroying everything in His wrath), and another which heals some men's souls. If we take the first view, we cannot make sense of Christ's teachings concerning eternal judgment. This leaves us only the second view.

Why do we believe that there can be progress, in time and on earth, before the final judgment? Not because Christ is coming back physically to rapture His saints, and then to set up a millennial kingdom. There will be a rapture, but it will take place on the day of final judgment (I Corinthians 15:23-24). We believe in the *progressive healing of the world* because Christ died for this world. His death was not in vain.

If Christ died to save the souls of *all* men, yet many perish, then His death *was* partially in vain. But He *didn't* die to save the *souls* of all men.

For further study: Num. 14:21; Ps. 22:27-31; 72:19; Isa. 11:9; 27:6; Zech. 14:9; Heb. 8:11.

Recommended Reading
(an asterisk marks outstanding works)

*Alexander, J. A. *The Prophecies of Isaiah*. Reprint edition; Grand Rapids: Zondervan, 1953. (mid-19th century)

_____ . *The Psalms Translated and Explained*. Grand Rapids: Baker, 1975.

*Allis, Oswald T. *Prophecy and the Church*. Philadelphia: Presbyterian and Reformed, 1945. This is the most comprehensive critique of dispensationalism available, written by a postmillennialist who is often assumed to be an amillennialist.

*Boettner, Loraine. *The Millennium*. Philadelphia: Presbyterian and Reformed, 1957. Better in its critique of dispensationalism than its description of postmillennialism. Inadequate treatment of amillennialism.

Brown, David. *Christ's Second Coming: Will It Be Premillennial?* Reprint edition; Grand Rapids: Baker, 1983. (Same Brown as in Jamison, Fawcett & Brown; late 19th century.)

*Campbell, Roderick. *Israel and the New Covenant*. Reprint edition; Tyler, TX: Geneva Divinity School Press, (1954) 1981. Probably the best one-volume exegetical treatment of postmillennialism.

*Chilton, David. *Paradise Restored*. Ft. Worth, TX: Dominion Press, 1984. Available from the Institute for Christian Economics, Tyler, TX.

_____ . *The Days of Vengeance*. Ft. Worth, TX: Dominion Press, 1987. Available from the Institute for Christian Economics, Tyler, TX.

_____ . *The Great Tribulation*. Ft. Worth, TX: Dominion Press, 1987. Available from the Institute for Christian Economics, Tyler, TX.

Custance, Arthur. *The Seed of the Woman*. P.O. Box 291, Brockville, Ontario, Canada K6V 5V5. Excellent on the question of life expectancy.

Hodge, A. A. *Evangelical Theology*. Edinburgh: Banner of Truth, 1976, chapters 12-14.

de Jong, J. A. *As the Waters Cover the Sea: Millennial expectations in the rise of Anglo-American missions, 1640-1810*. Kampen, Netherlands: J. H. Kok, 1970.

*Kik, J. Marcellus. *An Eschatology of Victory*. Nutley, NJ: Presbyterian and Reformed, 1971.

McPherson, Dave. *The Great Rapture Hoax*. 91 Lytle Rd, Fletcher, NC: New Puritan Library, 1983. A post-tribulation dispensationalist blows the whistle on who *really* invented the pretribulation rapture—and it wasn't J. N. Darby.

_____ . *The Incredible Cover-Up*. P.O. Box 4130, Medford, OR: Omega Publications, 1980. More evidence on the real origins of the pretribulation rapture doctrine.

Moore, T. V. *A Commentary on Haggai, Zechariah and Malachi*. Edinburgh: Banner of Truth, 1960.

Murray, Iain. *The Puritan Hope: A Study in Revival and the Interpretation of Prophecy*. London: Banner of Truth, 1971.

North, Gary. *Backward, Christian Soldiers?* Tyler, TX: Institute for Christian Economics, 1984. Practical rather than exegetical.

_____ . *Dominion and Common Grace*. Tyler, TX: Institute for Christian Economics, 1987.

_____ . *Unconditional Surrender: God's Program for Victory*. 3rd edition; Ft. Worth, TX: Dominion Press, 1988. Part III. Available from the Institute for Christian Economics, Tyler, TX.

_____ , ed. *The Journal of Christian Reconstruction*, Vol. III, No. 2: Symposium on the Millennium. (This journal is published by the Chalcedon Foundation, P.O. Box 158, Vallecito, CA 95251.)

_____, ed. *The Journal of Christian Reconstruction*, Vol. VIII, No. 1: Symposium on Social Action.

_____, ed. *Christianity & Civilization*, No. 2: The Theology of Christian Resistance. (This journal is published by Geneva Ministries, Box 131300, Tyler, TX 75713.) Available from the Institute for Christian Economics, Tyler, TX.

_____, ed. *Christianity & Civilization*, No. 3: The Tactics of Christian Resistance. Available from the Institute for Christian Economics, Tyler, TX.

Rose, Tom, and Robert Metcalf. *The Coming Victory*. Memphis: Christian Studies Center, 1980.

Rushdoony, Rousas John. *God's Plan for Victory: The Meaning of Postmillennialism*. Tyler, TX: Thoburn Press, 1980.

_____. *Thy Kingdom Come: Studies in Daniel and Revelation*. Tyler, TX: Thoburn Press, 1978.

Terry, Milton S. *Biblical Hermeneutics*. Grand Rapids: Zondervan Publishing House, 1984.

Warfield, Benjamin B. *Biblical and Theological Studies*. Philadelphia: Presbyterian and Reformed, 1968.

*Wilson, Dwight. *Armageddon Now! — The Premillenarian Response to Russia and Israel Since 1917*. Grand Rapids: Baker Book House, 1977. A delight to read. Erroneous, crackpot predictions for 60 years from famous religious leaders who were absolutely confident in their predictions! Available from the Institute for Christian Economics, Tyler, TX.

Conclusion

Well, what is *your* conclusion? I will assume that you have read the entire book to this point. I can think of several possible conclusions you might have come to:

1. All 75 questions are invalid.
2. Some of the 75 questions are valid.
3. All of the 75 questions are valid.
4. I'm not sure of anything any more.
5. I don't want to think about any of this.

I suspect that anyone who has read all 75 questions and "questionable answers" will not select conclusion number five. The majority of people who began this book probably already did select number five, and put away this book long ago. But for those of you who remain, one of the first four conclusions is more likely.

For those of you who conclude that all 75 questions are invalid and misleading, I can only thank you for staying with me this far. I've done my best; I just didn't persuade you. Maybe the timing isn't right. Maybe next year you'll be ready to reconsider. Or maybe I'm just plain wrong. But you did give me a hearing, and for this I'm thankful. Not many people are willing to give a hearing to the controversial opinions in this book.

For those of you who think that some of the questions are valid, I suggest that you figure out why you believe in some of them but not all of them. If I have changed your mind concerning one entire section—Part One, Two, or Three—but not another, then you have two responsibilities: keep on reading in the field you agree with, and continue studying the field you don't agree with. You have to come up with solid biblical reasons why I have completely missed the point in one area while hitting the target in another one. Unquestionably, you need to become an expert in the field you do agree with, because you're going to be "under the gun" from your friends and institutional superiors from now on.

If you agree with some questions within a section, but not others, you had better find out which of us is being inconsistent: you or I. It's difficult for me to believe that each of the three sections isn't internally self-consistent, but maybe I'm wrong. Keep studying.

For anyone who is just confused, you had better keep thinking about these questions until you get "unconfused," one way or another.

If You Agree With the 75 Questions

Now, for those of you who are convinced that my case in all three areas is essentially correct, you are in trouble. You have now adopted theological positions which are decidedly out of favor—*hated* might be closer to it—by the vast majority of those who call themselves Christians. (As for the opinion of humanists, you are officially "off the wall.")

You now have a number of responsibilities. First, you must recognize that you have been given knowledge which few Christians in our day have ever heard about, let alone considered. Most of your peers will disagree with you, including those few who have seen or even read this book. Second, with greater knowledge comes added responsibility: **"For unto whomsoever much is given, of him shall be much required"**

(Luke 12:48).

What are some of these responsibilities? Before I discuss this question, let me briefly describe what these responsibilities are not: to be louder, pushier, less patient with the opinions of others, and unwilling to do a *lot* more reading before you publicly express your new opinions. In short, your responsibility is to avoid becoming a *red hot*. Nobody wants or appreciates unpopular opinions from a red hot. Cool off before you mouth off.

If you agree with the 75 questions, you may be lured into joining what is sometimes called the IBM syndrome: *"I've been misled!"* Yes, you have undoubtedly been misled. Furthermore, there are people who will do everything possible to mislead you some more. But your problem is now educational: to become so familiar with the Bible that you cannot easily be misled in the future. You must *master* the Bible, as you have never thought of mastering it in the past. You must devote yourself to a full understanding of the whole counsel of God. You must do a vastly better job in understanding Christianity than those who have misled you have understood it.

But that's only the beginning. You must begin to apply in your life what you've learned. **"But be ye doers of the word, and not hearers only, deceiving your own selves"** (James 1:22). It's not just a matter of knowing more than your peers, let alone your instructors. It's a matter of outperforming them. Not only must you think more clearly than they do, you must also act more consistently than they do. *By your fruits shall they know you.*

If you're enrolled at some school, you have to become a better student—a fully self-disciplined student. Your new faith must reflect itself in better academic performance if you're in school, or better job performance if you're not in school. You have got to demonstrate by your performance in every area of life that not only is your theology different, but that *it makes a difference*. You've got to do better than the vast majority of your competitors.

Sure, you've been misled in the past. So don't mislead others. This means that you have to know what you're talking about. If you were to memorize every word in this little book, you would barely have scratched the surface. The difference between what you believe today compared with what you have been taught in the past is undoubtedly tremendous. But that difference has to become even greater. We haven't even begun to talk about such questions as epistemology (what do we know and how can we know it), apologetics (the intellectual defense of the faith), applied theology (Christian economics, Christian psychology, Christian education, Christian politics, etc.), church government, the sacraments, missions, and the growing problem of Christian resistance to tyranny. So *you've only just begun*, as the early 1970's song said.

On what grounds should you assume a position of arrogance? None. Compared with what's ahead, if you really get serious about your Christian faith, what you've accomplished so far is pretty minimal. You've read one little book, and an easy one at that. Compared with what the church as a whole is required by God to accomplish, you've barely taken your first steps.

This isn't to say that you're not ahead of those who previously misled you. You're way, way ahead. It's only that compared with what still needs to be accomplished—by you, by the church as a whole, and by

Christian civilization—the distance between you and those who misled you really isn't very meaningful.

That's why you have to have a good attitude. If you've got a better grip on the truth than they do—and you do—then prove it, not by your contentiousness, but by your performance in your calling (whatever it is that God has called you to). If your new world and life view doesn't manifest itself in vastly improved performance on your part, then you're just a tinkling cymbal, sounding brass (I Corinthians 13:1). Read all of I Corinthians 13 before you think too well of yourself. Then read II Peter 1:5-10.

On the other hand, don't become a shrinking violet. Your job isn't to become an intellectual doormat. There are too many of them around as it is. If someone asks you what you believe, tell him. If he challenges your biblical understanding, be prepared politely and graciously to bury him with Bible citations and arguments. Your task is not to be arrogant, but so well prepared that you utterly crush your opponents theologically. **"But sanctify the Lord God in your hearts: and be ready always to give an answer to every man that asketh you a reason of the hope that is in you with meekness and fear"** (I Peter 3:15). Understand that this meekness and fear is supposed to be meekness and fear of *God*, not of men.

Never forget, this technique of burying your questioner is supposed to be a *response*. The text says that you must be prepared *to answer* any person who asks you. The tactic requires that you patiently *wear out your opponent*. Be thoroughly prepared biblically to respond to him every time he says, "Yes, but. . . ." If he didn't ask, tread lightly. If he stops saying, "Yes, but. . . ." you should stop trying to bury him.

Don't keep badgering people, especially professors.

If they refuse to acknowledge the truth of what the Bible teaches, that's their problem, not yours. Ask one question, and limit yourself at most to one follow-up response, or else you will alienate other students and the professor. Furthermore, if your professor scoffs at the legitimacy of your questions, keep in mind Jesus' words concerning scoffers (and, by implication, concerning vindictive instructors who will try to get even by flunking you, publicly humiliating you, or by expelling you): "**Give not that which is holy unto the dogs, neither cast ye your pearls before swine, lest they trample them under their feet, and turn again and rend you**" (Matthew 7:6).

In short, your job isn't to become a sacrificial lamb for those who have systematically misled you and your peers. *Your job is to do everything you can to* **undo the damage** *they have done*. You will have to devote the rest of your life to this task. The place to begin is right where you are. The time to begin is tomorrow, if not sooner. You are now ready, as they say, "to get with the program." The program is outlined in the following appendices. And if it sounds like too great a task, go to the library (or send $4 to the Notre Dame University Press in Notre Dame, Indiana) and get a copy of Douglas Hyde's book, *Dedication and Leadership*. Hyde was an ex-Communist who became a Christian. He shows the kinds of sacrifices that the Communists have been ready to make in order to achieve their goals. Christians should be no less dedicated. They should be even more dedicated. If anyone is going to take you seriously in the future, you had better be ready to begin to apply the self-discipline program outlined by Hyde. You had also better be ready to teach others. Read the following two appendices and get to work. You have been given much; much is now expected from you in return.

Appendix A
How to Get Your Answers

This section is aimed at college students who attend a Christian college. It could also apply to high school students. To a lesser degree, it can apply to people in a church Bible study, but as you will see, there are differences between a Bible study and a formal classroom situation, where the rules for discussion are more rigid.

On the assumption that you're a college student, you should consider the following observations. You're paying money to get good questions asked and hard questions answered. By remaining in school, you're forfeiting the income you might be earning if you dropped out (which I don't recommend). You're in one school and not another. This involves costs; the other school might be better (I doubt it, however). One of the benefits that college is supposed to provide is an atmosphere of learning, which unquestionably involves getting instructors to help you answer your questions.

Any attempt on the part of instructors to keep questions from being raised is highly suspicious. An outright ban on Bible questions in a Christian school is an admission of intellectual bankruptcy on the part of your college's administration. They are stealing your tuition money unless they admit openly that students are not entitled to ask fundamental theological and philosophical questions. But this admission must be public and in writing for all to see. Anything less is subterfuge; *they are stealing your money*. They are also probably lying to you about other matters, too. (Some of you who attend more intellectually rigorous campuses may not believe that students can be expelled at some big-name Christian colleges for the mere possession of a book like this, but it's true.)

Guidelines

Nevertheless, administrations and teachers can establish certain guidelines concerning how questions may be raised, and under what circumstances. They are not morally bound to answer each and every question which any student may want to ask on any given day. So students must exercise discretion.

To help you exercise discretion, I have devised a set of rules or general guidelines for asking questions in an open, academically acceptable, and morally proper manner. Students who strive to abide by these rules should experience success, *if their instructors are intellectually honest people*. These are not absolutely rigid rules, but they are highly suggested.

There are definite restrictions on what can be considered proper in a classroom, and to violate classroom decorum is to alienate both teachers and fellow students. It should not be your goal to alienate anyone as a result of your behavior. Your questions may well alienate people, but that is always the risk when people begin to inquire about questions of truth and falsehood, especially when openly religious issues are at stake.

You must recognize your status. Status must not be ignored. You're restricted by the following considerations:

1. Your age.
2. Your lack of experience.
3. Your lack of self-confidence.
4. Your subordinate position (student).
5. Your fellow students.
6. The rules of classroom discussion.
7. The rules of the school regarding theology.
8. Your position as a Christian.
9. Your ability to communicate effectively.

Let us consider these one by one.

1. *Your Age*

There are basic rules of behavior when younger people confront their elders. **"Likewise, ye younger, submit yourselves unto the elder. Yea, all of you be subject one to another, and be clothed with humility: for God resisteth the proud, and giveth grace to the humble"** (I Peter 5:5). The reference is to the church office of elder, but the general principle is applicable outside of the institutional church. Again, **"Thou shalt rise up before the hoary head, and honour the face of the old man, and fear thy God: I am the LORD"** (Leviticus 19:32). There can be little doubt that God expects younger people to respect the status position of the older person. The older person is not to abuse this position of authority, but even if he does, younger people must exercise restraint. Not blind submission, but restraint.

Those who flagrantly disobey this commandment are unlikely to achieve success in any field for very long. If nothing else, as they grow old, younger people will treat them similarly. Men reap what they sow. No righteous cause is furthered by disobeying God's ethical standards.

Others around you will lose respect for you if you tread heavily on the toes of older people. Treading lightly is permissible in some instances; God does not honor their stupidity or incompetence indefinitely. But open defiance leads to trouble in the classroom.

2. *Your Lack of Experience*

It takes time in most academic disciplines to gain experience. Certain fields are apparently exempt from this rule: advanced mathematics, theoretical physics, and perhaps certain forms of symbolic philosophy. A person who has not made a major contribution in higher mathematics by age 30 is probably unlikely to make one later on. Yet only a handful of very bright people escape the general rule regarding experience, even in higher mathematics. In those disciplines in which these questions will prove relevant, experience counts for a great deal.

We must not ignore the cumulative effects of years of study, difficult personal experiences, and years of hearing sermons. The Bible is a complex and difficult book. It's so subtle that no wise man can say that he has mastered it, although fools may assert that they have. So you should take seriously the opposing viewpoint of someone who has studied the Bible over many years.

Nevertheless, experience has its limits. Perhaps the person has had experience, but has not interpreted this experience accurately in terms of biblical revelation. Cumulative error offers no advantages; cumulative accuracy does.

There should be growth in the faith, including applied Christianity, over a lifetime. This is the doctrine of *progressive sanctification*. It applies to academic matters as much as it applies anywhere else. Younger people must give the benefit of the doubt to those whose age indicates that they may possess experience. (And for people who should have gained it, but haven't, there are techniques to offset their initial advantage, as I shall discuss later.)

3. *Your Lack of Self-Confidence*

This may not apply to you. Perhaps you're supremely confident. If you are, please reread the previous two sections. But for those of you who have doubts about yourself, understand how your doubts can affect your ability to ask questions and pursue answers.

You may not really understand your question. You may not understand its full implications. You may be "in over your head," or think you are. A question asked aggressively, when you're not really confident about your grasp of the issue, could lead to your capitulation and retreat in the face of a determined answer. Your teacher may recognize your hesitation. He may make you appear foolish, or overly aggressive, or ill-prepared. It never pays to appear to have lost an exchange of ideas. Better to structure your questions so that you cannot visibly lose.

In a hard-fought exchange, an experienced teacher will smell blood early. He will go for your weak points. Your fellow students will seldom come to your defense, unless you're known to be very shy or not too bright. Better to ask your questions in such a manner that your initial defeat will produce sympathy for you, and not hostility.

4. *Your Subordinate Position*

You're not simply younger and less experienced than your instructor. You're also *functionally subordinate*. He assigns grades; you receive grades. He has lawful authority to a very great degree over the activities of his classroom. The college has granted him this authority. Indirectly, your parents have, too, unless you're totally independent financially. You have agreed, implicitly or explicitly, to follow certain rules of behavior when you entered college and entered the classroom. This is a covenant which must be honored. Therefore, the sense of authority which is to put fear in men's hearts is operative. You're at a psychological disadvantage whenever you confront this authority directly. You must do so very subtly.

5. *Your Fellow Students*

Students recognize their subordinate position. Any student who begins to take an aggressive stance risks being labeled "uppity" by other students, who see him as someone who is attempting to exercise authority which others know they don't legitimately possess. "Who does he think he is, anyway?" is a question which can undermine a student's real goal, which is to get his questions answered, or to persuade other students of the truth of his position.

Furthermore, other students pay their tuitions, too. They come to class to learn, and this usually means learning from the instructor. He knows this, and he can subtly manipulate student opinion against those who tie up the class.

On the other hand, if you develop the ability to ask relevant questions concerning issues that are bothering other students, you can act as their surrogate.

You take the consequences if there are any. You may wind up looking stupid, not them, and they still get their question answered. So if you serve as a kind of intermediary between the instructor and your equally confused fellow students, no one is likely to get angry.

You must learn to assess their response. Part of your responsibility is to keep from alienating them. You want to uphold a cause, even if that cause is the legitimacy of asking probing, controversial questions. You must not abuse the privilege you have of being able to ask an instructor questions. Use it to your advantage, and the advantage of other students. But retreat from any direct confrontation unless other students want to join in the fray on your side.

They did not pay to hear your ideas. They paid to hear the instructor's ideas. Only if you help them understand the implications of what he is saying are you likely to impress them with your position.

6. *The Rules of Classroom Discussion*

Different professors prefer different teaching methods. Some like to lecture without any interruptions. Others prefer a "Socratic method" of questions. Some permit a mixture. Be careful not to violate the familiar procedure of the classroom. But be warned: an instructor who refuses to take questions is usually extremely insecure intellectually. He is afraid. He may react in a very hostile manner if you in any way disturb his normal presentation. It may sound amazing to you now, but there are many teachers in classrooms who are barely able to get by academically. Tread carefully; the least competent instructor intellectually can be the most dangerous.

If there is no way to get questions answered in class,

why not ask him publicly if he would be willing to set aside an extra hour to answer some of the questions that you want answered? Maybe other students would like to attend. (It will pay you to scout around ahead of time and get several others to encourage him to set aside a special session for this purpose.) If he refuses, you *know* that you're facing a man who knows that he doesn't have the answers.

7. *The Rules of the School Regarding Theology*

Some schools have a strict statement of faith which students must sign. If you've signed it, you've done your duty. Now you're only thinking about certain problems that have come up. Just keep thinking. Who says you have to review that statement of faith each time you think of some new idea?

If the administration threatens you with expulsion if you don't re-sign ("re-sign or resign"), then you should refuse to sign, assuming you really have changed your mind. Make them put their threat in writing, and make them state it in front of a witness. If they refuse, and still expel you, you then have a major reason to appeal to the regional accrediting association.

Rule: *never, ever resign voluntarily*. Always force them to expel you. The evil act must be theirs. Don't capitulate in the face of evil. Besides, you can't prove much against them unless they actually expel you, in writing. And the day you've got that, you've got them.

8. *Your Position as a Christian*

Your actions testify to the God you serve. Generally, it's unwise for a student to pursue a matter with an instructor to the point of conflict. It's a bad testimony. When you simply cannot get straight answers from your instructors, after repeated attempts, your best strategy is to begin a private Bible study. (See the next chapter for details.) You must be courteous. There are other ways to get answers. Never become dependent on an instructor to give you all of your answers. Sometimes your conduct must override your desire to get "spoon-fed" answers from people who just don't have any. Politely go your own way and seek out other places to get answers.

9. *Your Ability to Communicate Effectively*

Very few people ever learn the skills of verbal argumentation. The person who does tends to seek employment in a position that allows him an advantage in this area. This may be your instructor. (Maybe not; there are some amazingly inept communicators who are in college classrooms—far more than first-semester freshmen realize.) The point is, you had better know your limitations before you attempt to get into a confrontation with an instructor. Better to avoid direct confrontations. There are many ways to skin a cat.

Student Resentment

Be forewarned: some students will resent your bringing up these questions. They have read them, and these questions have begun to create havoc in their spiritual lives. They resent these questions, for they present very different views of God, time, and ethics than are common in thousands of Christian churches. These questions are painful to them. Thus, they prefer to forget about them. They don't want to be reminded of the kind of God the Bible reveals. You will gain enemies if you pursue publicly the issues raised in this book. You must pursue them anyway, if you're morally honest. You must get answers. And if your instructors are unable to provide them, you must be satisfied in your mind that you have done your best to get answers.

Here are some of the reasons why some of your classmates and most of your faculty are disturbed by these questions:

A new view of *God* is presented.
A new view of *God's authority* is presented.
A new view of *God's judgment* is presented.
A new view of *personal responsibility* is presented.
A new view of *human depravity* is presented.
A new view of *the future* is presented.

This being the case, there are other very disturbing questions that come to mind:

Why wasn't I told about this before?
Was someone deliberately concealing these issues?
Is this really what the Bible teaches?
How can I determine what the Bible teaches?
Are there answers to these questions?
Where can I find valid answers?
Am I intellectually honest?
Will I believe the truth or a lie?
What will God do to me if I believe a lie?
How reliable are my present instructors?
What will new beliefs do to my plans?
What will they cost me to adopt?
Am I going to "sell out" the truth?
Can I believe the Bible?
Can I believe my instructors?

These are disturbing questions for students—perhaps as disturbing as the 75 original questions are to the faculty. A student who is not disturbed by any of this book's 75 questions is either incredibly mature and well-informed, or over-confident in his ability to answer them, or so ignorant of their implications that he should probably drop out of school and get a job, or perhaps he is simply not a Christian.

The Safest Approach

Perhaps very few of your fellow students have seen this book. Perhaps hundreds of them have. It makes a difference. If everyone is talking about them, it may be perfectly safe to ask a question in class. You're just another face in the crowd. But if hardly anyone is discussing them, your question will identify you as someone who reads "subversive literature."

A frontal attack on power seldom produces victories. It's far wiser to join the crowd of the "disturbed." Other students will be bothered by many of the 75 initial questions and their corollaries. Some of them will want answers, too. They just don't know what to think. So you can ask for them.

There are lots of questions to ask. You may have several years to get answers. Don't be in a hurry. Just take your time. See which instructors have some insights, and which ones start to dance. It's always a sight to see instructors dance the *free-will two-step*, dancing away from the hard questions, seeking to evade the obvious implications. (Usually those campuses that prohibit social dancing are staffed by instructors who are experienced theological dancers.)

Are other students asking different questions? So much the better. Are they asking them in some classes, but not in others? Then you can probably identify yourself as one of the "mentally disturbed." If there are enough "disturbed" students on campus, no one gets in trouble. But if no one is asking questions, you must proceed cautiously. You could be identified as a troublemaker. There are few troublemakers more dangerous in the eyes of a college administration than students who ask pointed, relevant questions that ill-equipped instructors find it difficult to answer adequately. It makes the administration look bad, since the administration *hired* these instructors.

Every effort must be made by you to *avoid causing trouble by your tone of voice, your attitude, or your general conduct*. Your task is to get your questions answered—you're paying for this service—but not to get tossed out of school for being a smart alec.

Maybe you have come to grips with the implications of the 75 questions. You're satisfied that the questions are proper, and that the "Questionable Answers" will not withstand biblical evidence. My suggestion to you, with respect to the proper way to ask your questions, is this: ". . . **be ye therefore wise as serpents, and harmless as doves**" (Matthew 10:16b). You may already have made up your mind: you no longer believe in the theological position taught on your campus. You want to get answers if there are any, but you also are perfectly willing to expose your instructors before other students as men without valid answers. Your approach in the classroom should not be noticeably different from the person who just doesn't know what to make of all these questions, but who desperately wants valid answers for his or her peace of mind.

The safe approach is simple, and much simpler if many students are reading this book: "Sir, I was given a copy of a book called *75 Bible Questions*, and I really don't know how to deal with one of them. Have you thought about it?"

I guarantee you: this book has forced him to think about it. He may not have appealing answers, but he has thought about it. Or if he hasn't this week, he will have thought about it by next week. The more people who read this book, the more he will think about all 75 questions.

Another approach: "Sir, someone I was talking with raised a question I can't answer. Can you answer it?"

What if they want to know who asked you? Don't say. Protect that person. Is there persecution coming? The important issue is the question, not the person who brought up the question. An inquisition by the administration would be stupid on their part, but administrations are not always noted for their wisdom when dealing with certain kinds of student activities.

Even better is a question which relates directly—or can be made to seem to relate directly—to the lecture topic of the day. The question just pops into your head. Who can complain? (Your instructor, but he may not want to, since it will appear that he is intellectually incapable of dealing with the hard questions.)

It's almost always safer for women to ask hard questions than for men to ask. It's assumed by most male instructors that female students are not normally ready to get involved in a controversial issue that will create turbulence in the classroom. Some brighter women may have gained a reputation for challenging instructors, and for them there is no safety in gender. But normally quiet women can ask the hardest questions imaginable, since it will not be perceived by the instructor as a potentially aggressive or hostile act. This is a good reason for inquiring male students to get some woman to raise some of these questions in class. Any male student who can find a sweet, attractive woman—masculine instructors always appreciate attractive women—with a B average or better, and who sees the implications of these questions, should do his best to get her to: 1) ask some really tough questions in class over the semester; and 2) marry him when he can afford it—or maybe even sooner. (Getting married teaches people how to afford things, or at least do without things happily.)

"Stonewalling"

This word became popular after it was learned that President Nixon had told his associates to "stonewall" all questions. You may see a lot of stonewalling in your college career.

You ask your question. You get evasion. What then? Pursue? "Go for the throat"? Quit? Ask the same question next week? What?

The safest bet is to ask one—repeat, *one*—follow-up corollary to the original question. You just need "a little clarification." This is always the best tactic if the question arises naturally in the course of a lecture. Anyone can use more clarification. After all, a related question might appear on an exam sometime. Anyone in class can appreciate the fact that you're having trouble understanding.

If you get another equally evasive or clearly incorrect answer, drop it. You can quit. Or you can say, "Well, I just don't see how that relates to the problem, but I don't want to take up any more class time." You're being considerate to the other students. You also have made it appear that Dr. Stonewall is unable to handle tough questions. You have made your point.

If you try to pursue it, you will unquestionably alienate other students. If no one else wants to chime in, drop it. There is always another class and 74 other questions.

Be careful not to have a two-man team asking too many questions. The more students who get involved, the better. It's always harder to stonewall half a dozen people who are asking questions than only one or two. *Never give the impression that you're ganging up on an instructor.* This always backfires.

Remember: *the **smarter students** on campus will generally see the importance of these questions*. They may take a different view from yours, but they will understand why these questions should not produce professorial stonewalling. If there are no other students in class who are willing to ask these questions, then either they are afraid, or not very bright, or bored, or convinced that this particular instructor gets stuck for an answer when someone says "hello" to him. So drop it. For now.

"I Want You To Read . . ."

If your instructor begins to feel the heat, he may call you aside and ask you to read this or that rebuttal. If so, do what he says. If he is trying to answer your question, then you owe it to him to follow up. Read his recommended book.

I can say this with very little fear. *I have seen most of these answers.* You need to see what passes for biblical scholarship in some of these books. You will be astounded at the amount of evasion—*printed evasion*—of the issues. These are the "dancing instructors" for *your* instructors. It will do you a world of intellectual good to sit down and see just how weak the answers of their "best and brightest" really are. Be sure to compare the book or book section recommended by your instructor with the materials I recommend at the end of each section. See which makes more sense. See which conforms to the biblical text more closely.

Once you have read the recommended book, you

have a perfect right to come back to him in private with a written list of a dozen more questions that were raised in your mind by the recommended book. What about this? What about that? If the author believes this, then he has to believe thus and so. But thus and so isn't taught in the Bible. In fact, its opposite is explicitly taught. Is there anything else you can read? Does he have any answers of his own? If you have written up good questions, with Bible citations, you're reasonably well covered. And now stonewalling becomes almost impossible. As Nixon's senior staff man Haldeman so aptly put it, "When the toothpaste is out of the tube, it's almost impossible to get it back in." Your instructor has already hit you with his big guns. He is now totally on the defensive.

Conclusion

It's easier to get these questions answered in Bible classes than in electrical engineering. The social sciences and history lend themselves better to a discussion of basic theological issues than the hard sciences do. A class in philosophy should get these questions answered; if it doesn't, then there is something wrong with the class.

To repeat: the best way to get a question answered is when a related issue comes up in class during a lecture. This is why you should master the questions and think about their implications and applications. They are worth mastering, after all. And they do have enormous implications and applications.

Appendix B
What Are Biblical Blueprints?

How many times have you heard this one?

"The Bible isn't a textbook of . . ."

You've heard it about as many times as you've heard this one:

"The Bible doesn't provide blueprints for . . ."

The odd fact is that some of the people who assure you of this are Christians. Nevertheless, if you ask them, "Does the Bible have answers for the problems of life?" you'll get an unqualified "yes" for an answer.

Question: If the Bible isn't a textbook, and if it doesn't provide blueprints, then just how, specifically and concretely, does it provide answers for life's problems? Either it answers real-life problems or it doesn't.

In short: *Does the Bible make a difference*?

Let's put it another way. If a mass revival at last hits this nation, and if millions of people are regenerated by God's grace through faith in the saving work of Jesus Christ at Calvary, will this change be visible in the way the new converts run their lives? Will their politics change, their business dealings change, their families change, their family budgets change, and their church membership change?

In short: Will conversion make a visible difference in our personal lives? If not, why not?

Second, two or three years later, will Congress be voting for a different kind of defense policy, foreign relations policy, environmental policy, immigration policy, monetary policy, and so forth? Will the federal budget change? If not, why not?

In short: Will conversion to Christ make a visible difference in our civilization? If not, why not?

The Great Commission

What the Biblical Blueprints Series is attempting to do is to outline what some of that visible difference in our culture ought to be. The authors are attempting to set forth, in clear language, *fundamental biblical principles* in numerous specific areas of life. The authors are not content to speak in vague generalities. These books not only set forth explicit principles that are found in the Bible and derived from the Bible, they also offer specific practical suggestions about what things need to be changed and how Christians can begin programs that will produce these many changes.

The authors see the task of American Christians just as the Puritans who came to North America in the 1630's saw their task: *to establish a city on a hill* (Matthew 5:14). The authors want to see a biblical reconstruction of the United States, so that it can serve as an example to be followed all over the world. They believe that God's principles are tools of evangelism to bring the nations to Christ. The Bible promises us that these principles will produce such good fruit that the whole world will marvel (Deuteronomy 4:5-8). When nations begin to marvel, they will begin to soften to the message of the gospel. What the authors are calling for is *comprehensive revival*—a revival that will transform everything on earth.

APPENDIX B: WHAT ARE BIBLICAL BLUEPRINTS?

In other words, the authors are calling Christians to obey God and take up the Great Commission: to *disciple* (discipline) all the nations of the earth (Matthew 28:19).

What each author argues is that there are God-required principles of thought and practice in areas that some people today believe to be outside the area of "religion." What Christians should know by now is that *nothing* lies outside religion. God is judging all of our thoughts and acts, judging our institutions, and working through human history to bring this world to a final judgment.

We present the case that God offers *comprehensive salvation*—regeneration, healing, restoration, and the obligation of total social reconstruction—because the world is in *comprehensive sin*.

To judge the world it is obvious that God has to have standards. If there were no absolute standards, there could be no earthly judgment and no final judgment because men could not be held accountable.

(Warning: these next few paragraphs are very important. They are the base of the entire Blueprints Series. It is important that you understand my reasoning. I really believe that if you understand it, you will agree with it.)

To argue that God's standards don't apply to everything is to argue that sin hasn't affected and infected everything. To argue that God's Word doesn't give us a revelation of God's requirements for us is to argue that we are flying blind as Christians. It is to argue that there are *zones of moral neutrality* that God will not judge, either today or at the day of judgment, because these zones somehow are *outside His jurisdiction*. In short, "no law—no jurisdiction."

But if God *does* have jurisdiction over the whole universe, which is what every Christian believes, then there must be universal standards by which God executes judgment. The authors of this series argue for God's *comprehensive judgment*, and we declare His *comprehensive salvation*. We therefore are presenting a few of His *comprehensive blueprints*.

The Concept of Blueprints

An architectural blueprint gives us the structural requirements of a building. A blueprint isn't intended to tell the owner where to put the furniture or what color to paint the rooms. A blueprint does place limits on where the furniture and appliances should be put—laundry here, kitchen there, etc.—but it doesn't take away our personal options based on personal taste. A blueprint just specifies what must be done during construction for the building to do its job and to survive the test of time. It gives direction to the contractor. Nobody wants to be on the twelfth floor of a building that collapses.

Today, we are unquestionably on the twelfth floor, and maybe even the fiftieth. Most of today's "buildings" (institutions) were designed by humanists, for use by humanists, but paid for mostly by Christians (investments, donations, and taxes). These "buildings" aren't safe. Christians (and a lot of non-Christians) now are hearing the creaking and groaning of these tottering buildings. Millions of people have now concluded that it's time to: (1) call in a totally new team of foundation and structural specialists to begin a complete renovation, or (2) hire the original contractors to make at least temporary structural modifications until we can all move to safer quarters, or (3) call for an emergency helicopter team because time has just about run out, and the elevators aren't safe either.

The writers of this series believe that the first option is the wise one: Christians need to rebuild the foundations, using the Bible as their guide. This view is ignored by those who still hope and pray for the third approach: God's helicopter escape. Finally, those who have faith in minor structural repairs don't tell us what or where these hoped-for safe quarters are or how humanist contractors are going to build them any safer next time.

Why is it that some Christians say that God hasn't drawn up any blueprints? If God doesn't give us blueprints, then who does? If God doesn't set the permanent standards, then who does? If God hasn't any standards to judge men by, then who judges man?

The humanists' answer is inescapable: *man* does—autonomous, design-it-yourself, do-it-yourself man. Christians call this man-glorifying religion the religion of humanism. It is amazing how many Christians until quite recently have believed humanism's first doctrinal point, namely, that God has not established permanent blueprints for man and man's institutions. Christians who hold such a view of God's law serve as *humanism's chaplains*.

Men are God's appointed "contractors." We were never supposed to draw up the blueprints, but we *are* supposed to execute them in history and then after the resurrection. Men have been given dominion on the earth to subdue it for God's glory. "So God created man in His own image; in the image of God He created him; male and female He created them. Then God blessed them, and God said to them, 'Be fruitful and multiply; fill the earth and subdue it; have dominion over the fish of the sea, over the birds of the air, and over every living thing that moves on the earth'" (Genesis 1:27-28).

Christians about a century ago decided that God never gave them the responsibility to do any building (except for churches). That was just what the humanists had been waiting for. They immediately stepped in, took over the job of contractor ("Someone has to do it!"), and then announced that they would also be in charge of drawing up the blueprints. We can see the results of a similar assertion in Genesis, chapter 11: the tower of Babel. Do you remember God's response to that particular humanistic public works project?

Never Be Embarrassed by the Bible

This sounds simple enough. Why should Christians be embarrassed by the Bible? But they *are* embarrassed . . . millions of them. The humanists have probably done more to slow down the spread of the gospel by convincing Christians to be embarrassed by the Bible than by any other strategy they have adopted.

Test your own thinking. Answer this question: "Is God mostly a God of love or mostly a God of wrath?" Think about it before you answer.

It's a trick question. The biblical answer is: "God is equally a God of love and a God of wrath." But Christians these days will generally answer almost automatically, "God is mostly a God of love, not wrath."

Now in their hearts, they know this answer can't be

true. God sent His Son to the cross to die. His own Son! That's how much God hates sin. That's wrath with a capital "W."

But why did He do it? Because He loves His Son, and those who follow His Son. So, you just can't talk about the wrath of God without talking about the love of God, and vice versa. The cross is the best proof we have: God is both wrathful and loving. Without the fires of hell as the reason for the cross, the agony of Jesus Christ on the cross was a mistake, a case of drastic overkill.

What about heaven and hell? We know from John's vision of the day of judgment, "Death and Hades [hell] were cast into the lake of fire. This is the second death. And anyone not found written in the Book of Life was cast into the lake of fire" (Revelation 20:14-15).

Those whose names are in the Book of Life spend eternity with God in their perfect, sin-free, resurrected bodies. The Bible calls this the New Heaven and the New Earth.

Now, which is more eternal, the lake of fire, or the New Heaven and the New Earth? Obviously, they are both eternal. So, God's wrath is equally ultimate with His love throughout eternity. *Christians all admit this*, but sometimes only under extreme pressure. And that is precisely the problem.

For over a hundred years, theological liberals have blathered on and on about the love of God. But when you ask them, "What about hell?" they start dancing verbally. If you press them, they eventually deny the existence of eternal judgment. We *must* understand: they have no doctrine of the total love of God because they have no doctrine of the total wrath of God. They can't really understand what it is that God in His grace offers us in Christ because they refuse to admit what eternal judgment tells us about the character of God.

The doctrine of eternal fiery judgment is by far the most unacceptable doctrine in the Bible, as far as hell-bound humanists are concerned. They can't believe that Christians can believe in such a horror. But we do. We must. This belief is the foundation of Christian evangelism. It is the motivation for Christian foreign missions. We shouldn't be surprised that the God-haters would like us to drop this doctrine. When Christians believe it, they make too much trouble for God's enemies.

So if we believe in this doctrine, the doctrine above all others that ought to embarrass us before humanists, then why do we start to squirm when God-hating people ask us: "Well, what kind of God would require the death penalty? What kind of God would send a plague (or other physical judgment) on people, the way He sent one on the Israelites, killing 70,000 of them, even though they had done nothing wrong, just because David had conducted a military census in peacetime (2 Samuel 24:10-16)? What kind of God sends AIDS?" The proper answer: "The God of the Bible, *my* God."

Compared to the doctrine of eternal punishment, what is some two-bit judgment like a plague? Compared to eternal screaming agony in the lake of fire, without hope of escape, what is the death penalty? The liberals try to embarrass us about these earthly "down payments" on God's final judgment because they want to rid the world of the idea of final judgment. So they insult the character of God, and also the character of Christians, by sneering at the Bible's account of who God is, what He has done in history, and what He requires from men.

Are you tired of their sneering? I know I am.

Nothing in the Bible should be an embarrassment to any Christian. We may not know for certain precisely how some biblical truth or historic event should be properly applied in our day, but every historic record, law, announcement, prophecy, judgment, and warning in the Bible is the very Word of God, and is not to be flinched at by anyone who calls himself by Christ's name.

We must never doubt that whatever God did in the Old Testament era, the Second Person of the Trinity also did. God's counsel and judgments are not divided. We must be careful not to regard Jesus Christ as a sort of "unindicted co-conspirator" when we read the Old Testament. "For whoever is ashamed of Me and My words in this adulterous and sinful generation, of him the Son of Man also will be ashamed when He comes in the glory of His Father with the holy angels" (Mark 8:38).

My point here is simple. If we as Christians can accept what is a very hard principle of the Bible, that Christ was a blood sacrifice for our individual sins, then we shouldn't flinch at accepting any of the rest of God's principles. As we joyfully accepted His salvation, so we must joyfully embrace all of His principles that affect any and every area of our lives.

The Whole Bible

When, in a court of law, the witness puts his hand on the Bible and swears to tell the truth, the whole truth, and nothing but the truth, so help him God, he thereby swears on the Word of God—the *whole* Word of God, and *nothing but* the Word of God. The Bible is a unit. It's a "package deal." The New Testament doesn't overturn the Old Testament; it's a *commentary* on the Old Testament. It tells us how to use the Old Testament properly in the period after the death and resurrection of Israel's messiah, God's Son.

Jesus said: "Do not think that I came to destroy the Law or the Prophets. I did not come to destroy but to fulfill. For assuredly, I say to you, till heaven and earth pass away, one jot or one tittle will by no means pass from the law till all is fulfilled. Whoever therefore breaks one of the least of these commandments, and teaches men to do so, shall be called least in the kingdom of heaven; but whoever does and teaches them, he shall be called great in the kingdom of heaven" (Matthew 5:17-19). The Old Testament isn't a discarded first draft of God's Word. It isn't "God's Word emeritus."

Dominion Christianity teaches that there are four covenants under God, meaning four kinds of *vows* under God: personal (individual), and the three institutional covenants: ecclesiastical (the church), civil (governments), and family. All other human institutions (business, educational, charitable, etc.) are to one degree or other under the jurisdiction of these four covenants. No single covenant is absolute; therefore, no single institution is all-powerful. Thus, Christian liberty is *liberty under God and God's law*.

Christianity therefore teaches pluralism, but a very special kind of pluralism: plural institutions under God's comprehensive law. It does not teach a pluralism of law structures or a pluralism of moralities, for as we will see shortly, this sort of ultimate pluralism (as distinguished from *institutional* pluralism) is always either polytheistic or humanistic. Christian people are required to take dominion over the earth by means of all these God-ordained institutions, not just the church, or just the state, or just the family. *The kingdom of God includes every human institution and every aspect of life, for all of life is under God and is governed by His unchanging principles.* All of life is under God and God's principles because God intends to *judge* all of life *in terms of* His principles.

In this structure of *plural governments*, the institutional churches serve as *advisors* to the other institutions (the Levitical function), but the churches can only pressure individual leaders through the threat of excommunication. As a restraining factor on unwarranted church authority, an unlawful excommunication by one local church or denomination is always subject to review by the others if and when the excommunicated person seeks membership elsewhere. Thus, each of the three covenantal institutions is to be run under God, as interpreted by its lawfully elected or ordained leaders, with the advice of the churches, not the compulsion.

Majority Rule

Just for the record, the authors aren't in favor of imposing some sort of top-down bureaucratic tyranny in the name of Christ. The kingdom of God requires a bottom-up society. The bottom-up Christian society rests ultimately on the doctrine of *self*-government under God. It's the humanist view of society that promotes top-down bureaucratic power.

The authors are in favor of evangelism and missions leading to a widespread Christian revival, so that the great mass of earth's inhabitants will place themselves under Christ's protection and voluntarily use His covenantal principles for self-government. Christian reconstruction begins with personal conversion to Christ and self-government under God's principles, then spreads to others through revival, and only later brings comprehensive changes in civil law when the vast majority of voters voluntarily agree to live under biblical blueprints.

Let's get this straight: Christian reconstruction depends on majority rule. Of course, the leaders of the Christian reconstructionist movement expect a majority eventually to accept Christ as savior. If this doesn't happen, then Christians must be content with only partial reconstruction and only partial blessings from God. It isn't possible to ramrod God's blessings from the top down, unless you're God. Only humanists think that man is God. All we're trying to do is get the ramrod away from them and melt it down. The melted ramrod could then be used to make a great grave marker for humanism: "The God That Failed."

The Continuing Heresy of Dualism

Many (of course, not all!) of the objections to the material in this book series will come from people who have a worldview that is very close to an ancient church problem: dualism. A lot of well-meaning Christian people are dualists, although they don't even know what it is.

Dualism teaches that the world is inherently divided: spirit vs. matter, or law vs. mercy, or mind vs. matter, or nature vs. grace. What the Bible teaches is that this world is divided *ethically* and *personally*: Satan vs. God, right vs. wrong. The conflict between God and Satan will end at the final judgment. Whenever

Christians substitute some other form of dualism for ethical dualism, they fall into heresy and suffer the consequences. That's what has happened today. We are suffering from revived versions of ancient heresies.

Marcion's Dualism

The Old Testament was written by the same God who wrote the New Testament. There were not two Gods in history, meaning there was no dualism or radical split between the two testamental periods. There is only one God, in time and eternity.

This idea has had opposition throughout church history. An ancient two-Gods heresy was first promoted in the church about a century after Christ's crucifixion, and the church has always regarded it as just that, a heresy. It was proposed by a man named Marcion. Basically, this heresy teaches that there are two completely different law systems in the Bible: Old Testament law and New Testament law (or non-law). But Marcion took the logic of his position all the way. He argued that two law systems means two Gods. The God of wrath wrote the Old Testament, and the God of mercy wrote the New Testament. In short: "two laws — two Gods."

Many Christians still believe something dangerously close to Marcionism: not a two-Gods view, exactly, but a God-who-changed-all-His-rules sort of view. They begin with the accurate teaching that the ceremonial laws of the Old Testament were fulfilled by Christ and therefore that the *unchanging principles* of biblical worship are *applied differently* in the New Testament. But then they erroneously conclude that the whole Old Testament system of civil law was dropped by God, and *nothing biblical was put in its place*. In other words, God created a sort of vacuum for state law.

This idea turns civil law-making over to Satan. In our day, this means that civil law-making is turned over to humanists. *Christians have unwittingly become the philosophical allies of the humanists with respect to civil law.* With respect to their doctrine of the state, therefore, most Christians hold what is in effect a two-Gods view of the Bible.

Gnosticism's Dualism

Another ancient heresy that is still with us is gnosticism. It became a major threat to the early church almost from the beginning. It was also a form of dualism, a theory of a radical split. The gnostics taught that the split is between evil matter and good spirit. Thus, their goal was to escape this material world through other-worldly exercises that punish the body. They believed in *retreat from the world of human conflicts and responsibility*. Some of these ideas got into the church, and people started doing ridiculous things. One "saint" sat on a platform on top of a pole for several decades. This was considered very spiritual. (Who fed him? Who cleaned up after him?)

Thus, many Christians came to view "the world" as something permanently outside the kingdom of God. They believed that this hostile, forever-evil world cannot be redeemed, reformed, and reconstructed. Jesus didn't really die for it, and it can't be healed. At best, it can be subdued by power (maybe). This dualistic view of the world vs. God's kingdom narrowly restricted any earthly manifestation of God's kingdom. Christians who were influenced by gnosticism concluded that God's kingdom refers only to the institutional church. They argued that the institutional

APPENDIX B: WHAT ARE BIBLICAL BLUEPRINTS?

church is the *only* manifestation of God's kingdom.

This led to two opposite and equally evil conclusions. *First*, power religionists ("salvation through political power") who accepted this definition of God's kingdom tried to put the institutional church in charge of everything, since it is supposedly "the only manifestation of God's kingdom on earth." To subdue the supposedly unredeemable world, which is forever outside the kingdom, the institutional church has to rule with the sword. A single, monolithic institutional church then gives orders to the state, and the state must without question enforce these orders with the sword. The hierarchy of the institutional church concentrates political and economic power. *What then becomes of liberty?*

Second, escape religionists ("salvation is exclusively internal") who also accepted this narrow definition of the kingdom sought refuge from the evil world of matter and politics by fleeing to hide inside the institutional church, an exclusively "spiritual kingdom," now narrowly defined. They abandoned the world to evil tyrants. *What then becomes of liberty?* What becomes of the idea of God's progressive restoration of all things under Jesus Christ? What, finally, becomes of the idea of biblical dominion?

When Christians improperly narrow their definition of the kingdom of God, the visible influence of this comprehensive kingdom (both spiritual and institutional at the same time) begins to shrivel up. The first heresy leads to tyranny *by* the church, and the second heresy leads to tyranny *over* the church. Both of these narrow definitions of God's kingdom destroy the liberty of the responsible Christian man, self-governed under God and God's law.

Zoroaster's Dualism

The last ancient pagan idea that still lives on is also a variant of dualism: matter vs. spirit. It teaches that God and Satan, good and evil, are forever locked in combat and that good never triumphs over evil. The Persian religion of Zoroastrianism has held such a view for over 2,500 years. The incredibly popular "Star Wars" movies were based on this view of the world: the "dark" side of "the force" against its "light" side. In modern versions of this ancient dualism, the "force" is usually seen as itself impersonal: individuals personalize either the dark side or the light side by "plugging into" its power.

There are millions of Christians who have adopted a very pessimistic version of this dualism, though not in an impersonal form. God's kingdom is battling Satan's, and God's is losing. History isn't going to get better. In fact, things are going to get a lot worse externally. Evil will visibly push good into the shadows. The church is like a band of soldiers who are surrounded by a huge army of Indians. "We can't win boys, so hold the fort until Jesus comes to rescue us!"

That doesn't sound like Abraham, Moses, Joshua, Gideon, and David, does it? Christians read to their children one of the children's favorite stories, David and Goliath, yet in their own lives, millions of Christian parents really think that the Goliaths of this world are the unbeatable earthly winners. Christians haven't even picked up a stone.

Until very recently.

An Agenda for Victory

The change has come since 1980. Many Christians' thinking has shifted. Dualism, gnosticism, and "God

APPENDIX B: WHAT ARE BIBLICAL BLUEPRINTS?

changed His program midstream" ideas have begun to be challenged. The politicians have already begun to reckon with the consequences. Politicians are the people we pay to raise their wet index fingers in the wind to sense a shift, and they have sensed it. It scares them, too. It should.

A new vision has captured the imaginations of a growing army of registered voters. This new vision is simple: it's the old vision of Genesis 1:27-28 and Matthew 28:19-20. It's called *dominion*.

Four distinct ideas must be present in any ideology that expects to overturn the existing view of the world and the existing social order:

A doctrine of ultimate truth (permanence)
A doctrine of providence (confidence)
Optimism toward the future (motivation)
Binding comprehensive law (reconstruction)

The Marxists have had such a vision, or at least those Marxists who didn't live inside the bureaucratic giants called the Soviet Union and Red China. The radical (please, not "fundamentalist") Muslims of Iran also have such a view.

Now, for the first time in over 300 years, Bible-believing Christians have rediscovered these four points in the theology of Christianity. For the first time in over 300 years, a growing number of Christians are starting to view themselves as an army on the move. This army will grow. This series is designed to help it grow. And grow tougher.

The authors of this series are determined to set the agenda in world affairs for the next few centuries. We know where the permanent answers are found: in the Bible and *only* in the Bible. We believe that we have begun to discover at least preliminary answers to the key questions. There may be better answers, clearer answers, and more orthodox answers, but they must be found in the Bible, not at Harvard University or on the CBS Evening News.

We are self-consciously firing the opening shot. We are calling the whole Christian community to join with us in a very serious debate, just as Luther called them to debate him when he nailed the 95 theses to the church door over four and a half centuries ago.

It is through such an exchange of ideas by those who take the Bible seriously that a nation and a civilization can be saved. There are now 5 billion people in the world. If we are to win our world (and these billions of souls) for Christ we must lift up the message of Christ by becoming the city on the hill. When the world sees the blessings by God upon a nation run by His principles, the mass conversion of whole nations to the kingdom of our Lord will be the most incredible in of all history.

If we're correct about the God-required nature of our agenda, it will attract a dedicated following. It will produce a social transformation that could dwarf the Reformation. This time, we're not limiting our call for reformation to the institutional church.

This time, we mean business.

Unconditional Surrender:
God's Program for Victory
by Gary North

There is a war on. The war is between God and Satan. In our day, we see it most clearly in the conflicts between Christian institutions and the institutions of secular humanism. It is a war that is not going to go away. There will be a winner.

Unconditional Surrender is an introduction to this conflict. It covers the fundamental issues of the war: 1) What is the nature of *God?* 2) What is the nature of *man*? 3) What is the nature of *law?* If we can begin to answer these questions, then we will be able to recognize the nature of the battle.

Does Christianity make a difference in life? Does Christianity offer real-life solutions to the basic issues of life? Unquestionably, the answer is *yes*. But if we answer in the affirmative, then we have to start getting specific. Exactly how does Christianity make a difference? What kind of society would Christianity bring forth? What *practical* difference should Christianity make in the life of a ruler, businessman, judge, teacher, or scientist?

This book introduces people to the fundamentals of Christianity, including *applied* Christianity. It is thoroughly biblical and provides evidence taken directly from the Scriptures.

417 pp., indexed, bibliography, pb., $5.95
Institute for Christian Economics
P.O. Box 8000, Tyler, Texas 75711

Order all six of the books advertised here and receive a 40% discount.

Backward, Christian Soldiers?
An Action Manual for Christian Reconstruction
by Gary North

Jesus said to "Occupy till I come." But if Christians don't control the territory, they can't occupy it. They get tossed out into cultural "outer darkness," which is just exactly what the secular humanists have done to Christians in the 20th century: in education, in the arts, in entertainment, in politics, and certainly in the mainline churches and seminaries. Today, the humanists are "occupying." But they won't be for long. This book shows why.

For the first time in over a century, Christians are beginning to proclaim a seemingly new doctrine, yet the original doctrine was given to man by God: *dominion* (Genesis 1:28). But this doctrine implies another: *victory*. That's what this book is all about: *a strategy for victory*.

Satan may be alive on planet earth, but he's not well. He's in the biggest trouble he's been in since Calvary. If Christians adopt a *vision of victory* and a *program of Christian reconstruction*, we will see the beginning of a new era on earth: the kingdom of God manifested in every area of life. When Christ returns, Christians will be occupying, not hiding in the shadows, not sitting in the back of humanism's bus.

This book shows where to begin.

290 pp., indexed, pb., $5.95
Institute for Christian Economics
P.O. Box 8000, Tyler, Texas 75711

Order all six of the books advertised here and you receive a 40% discount.

Paradise Restored:
A Biblical Theology of Dominion
by David Chilton

In recent years many Christians have begun to realize a long forgotten truth: God wants us to have dominion over the earth, just as He originally commanded Adam and Eve. By His atonement, Jesus Christ has restored us to Adam's lost position, guaranteeing that God's original plan will be fulfilled. God will be glorified throughout the world: "*The earth shall be full of the knowledge of the LORD, as the waters cover the sea.*" Isaiah 11:9.

In order to demonstrate this truth from Scripture, David Chilton begins at the beginning, in the Garden of Eden. He shows how God established basic patterns in the first few chapters of Genesis – patterns which form the structure of later Biblical revelation. In the course of this book on eschatology, the reader is treated to an exciting, refreshingly *Biblical* way of reading the Bible.

Building on a solid foundation of New Testament eschatology, the author deals at length with the message of the Book of Revelation – often with surprising results. Throughout the volume, the reader is confronted with the fact that our view of the *future* is inescapably bound up with our view of Jesus Christ. According to the author, the fact that Jesus is *now* King of kings and Lord of lords means that His Gospel must be victorious: the Holy Spirit will bring the water of life to the ends of the earth. The Christian message is one of Hope.

342 pp., indexed, bibliography, pb., $17.95
Dominion Press, P.O. Box 8000, Tyler, Texas 75711

Order all six of the books advertised here and receive a 40% discount.

By This Standard
The Authority of God's Law Today
by Greg L. Bahnsen

God' Law or Chaos. God's Law or Tyranny. God's Law or God's Judgment. For over a century, most conservative Christian social thinkers and theologians have denied all three of these assertions. Some of them have even gone so far as to argue that God's law is inherently tyrannical. They have argued that the church can survive and even prosper under *any* legal order, except one: the rule of God's law. In this assertion, they join forces with secular humanists, occultists, and other assorted ethical rebels.

God's law is Christianity's tool of dominion. This is where any discussion of God's law ultimately arrives: the issue of *dominion*. Millions of Christians, sadly, have not recognized the continuing authority of God's law or its many applications to modern society. They have thereby reaped the whirlwind: cultural and intellectual impotence. They have surrendered this world to the devil. They have implicitly denied the power of the death and resurrection of Christ. They have served as footstools of the enemies of God. But humanism's free ride is coming to an end. This book serves as an introduction to this woefully neglected topic.

372 pp., indexed, pb., $4.95
Institute for Christian Economics
P.O. Box 8000, Tyler, Texas 75711

Order all six of the books advertised here and receive a 40% discount.

Millennialism and Social Theory
by Gary North

Will Jesus' Great Commission be fulfilled in history? Will God bring judgment against His enemies in history? Is there enough time for the healing power of the gospel to do its work? Two millennial views say no, there isn't enough time: premillennialism and amillennialism ("pessimillennialism"). A third view says yes, there is enough time: postmillennialism. By tying a vision of victory in history to the doctrine that the Bible offers specific answers to social problems, a new movement has begun to capture the minds of a generation of Christian activists. This movement is called Christian Reconstruction.

Millennialism and Social Theory presents a detailed critical account of how and why Protestant evangelicalism has retreated from the battlefields on which the war for modern man is being fought. it shows why Christian leaders have given up hope in the power of the gospel to transform societies as well as individual souls. It shows why Christianity is losing, and will continue to lose, as long as pessimillennialism is dominant. It also shows why this defeat is not inevitable, and why we can expect a great reversal.

393 pp., indexed, hb., $14.95
Institute for Christian Economics
P.O. Box 8000, Tyler, Texas 75711

Order all six of the books advertised here and receive a 40% discount.

Is the World Running Down?
Crisis in the Christian Worldview
by Gary North

This book is a creationist book. It is self-consciously anti-Darwin. It is not anti-science. The problem with modern humanistic science is that it presents a world-and-life view of inevitable despair. By tying man's origin to the evolution of an impersonal, uncreated universe, Charles Darwin tied man's destiny to the temporal fate of the impersonal universe. Modern physical science teaches that the galaxies will inevitably either die in the heat death of the universe or else crash back together to form a new "cosmic egg" that will explode into a new universe. In either case, all trace of man will disappear. The works of man's hands disappear forever. Life is swallowed up in death. What modern man needs is a message of hope. Modern humanistic science offers no hope to man, and neither does modern philosophy. Christianity offers hope because it rejects Darwinism and modern humanistic science. *Is The World Running Down?* is a manifesto of hope. It shows that creationists need not and must not cling to the humanists' view of entropy. It shows how recent social theory has been compromised by the entropy doctrine. It shows a way out: the doctrine of Christ's resurrection.

345 pages, indexed, hb., $19.95
Institute for Christian Economics
P.O. Box 8000, Tyler, TX 75711

Order all six of the books advertised here and receive a 40% discount.